A Young Person's Guide
to
Knowing God

A Young Person's Guide to Knowing God

Patricia St. John

CF4·K

To Rosy
to whom these
stories were first told

This editon © 2000
Reprinted 2008
ISBN:978-1-85792-558-6

Published by
Christian Focus Publications Ltd
Geanies House, Fearn,Tain, Ross-shire,
IV20 1TW, Scotland, U.K.
www.christianfocus.com
email: info@christianfocus.com

First published 1983 by Pickering & Inglis
Cover design by Daniel van Straaten
Printed and bound in Denmark
by Nørhaven Paperback A/S

Contents

Foreword

Patricia St. John had a special gift for storytelling, discovered in her early teens when each week she gathered up in the garage of her home the children of the neighbourhood. Patricia made Bible stories come alive in a way some of them still claim they have never forgotten. Later the street children in the mountain town in Morocco, where for some years she did medical work, gathered to hear Patricia's stories. When she retired it was the children of the housing estate where she lived in Coventry who crowded into her home in the evenings to play snooker and other games and to listen to a story before they left.

The stories in this book were told first at bedtime to her niece Rosy, now the mother of four small children. Since then the stories have been arranged to illustrate the different statements of the creed in a simple and effective way. A number of them are from Patricia's own experiences, others from history or legend.

Shortly before she died one headmaster wrote Patricia to tell her, 'I only wish you could have seen the 180 pairs of attentive eyes when I read your stories out in morning assembly. When the story reaches its climax the place is absolutely silent with rapt attention. Those of us who use your stories are so greatly in your debt.'

by Hazel St. John
1999

Questions answered in this book:

Who is God and what is he like? Does he care about me? Why is there so much suffering in the world? Why is Jesus called our 'Saviour'? Wasn't I born a Christian? What happens when I do wrong? Who is the Holy Spirit? Can I really know God?

Benefits of this book:

* Helps young people understand Christian doctrines.
* Encourages young people to know God for themselves.
* An ideal resource for School Assembly.
* Excellent resource for children's talks.
* Based on the Apostles' Creed.

THE APOSTLES' CREED

I believe in God the Father Almighty, Maker of heaven and earth;

And in Jesus Christ His only Son our Lord, Who was conceived by the Holy Ghost, Born of the Virgin Mary, Suffered under Pontius Pilate, Was crucified, dead and buried; He descended into hell; The third day he rose again from the dead; He ascended into heaven, And sitteth on the right hand of God the Father Almighty; From thence He shall come to judge the quick and the dead.

I believe in the Holy Ghost; The holy Catholic Church, The Communion of Saints; The Forgiveness of sins; The Resurrection of the body; And the Life everlasting.

AMEN

I BELIEVE IN GOD

... Who loves me as a Father
Luke 15:11–32

1. THE WHITE HANDKERCHIEF

The man sat on the pavement beside the bus stop, and stared at the stones. A few people turned to look at him - his unshaven face, his slumped shoulders, and his broken shoes; but he was not aware of their glances because he was reliving his life. He was no longer a hungry tramp who had slept last night under a railway arch; he was a boy who lived in a small red brick house up the next street, more than twenty years ago now. Perhaps they had bulldozed over the house by now; he hoped they hadn't crushed the pansies. It was strange how well he could remember the pansies, and the swing his dad had made for him, and the path where he had learned to ride his bike. They had saved up for months to buy that bike.

He shrugged impatiently, for the brightness of those pictures hurt him, and his memory travelled on another ten years. The bike had been exchanged for a motor cycle, and he then began to come home less often. He had a job by then and plenty of friends. Mum and dad seemed a bit sad and grey, and the pubs were a lot more fun. He did not really want to remember those years, nor the day when the debts had piled up, and he had gone home meaning to ask for money. They had made him a cup of tea and he had not liked to mention what he had come for. But he knew exactly where his dad kept the money, and later on, when they went out into the garden, it was quite easy to help himself to what he wanted.

That was the last time he had seen them. He had not wanted to go home again after that, and they had lost track of him. He had gone abroad and they knew nothing about the years of wandering nor the prison sentence. But locked in his cell at night he had thought a lot about them. Sometimes when he tossed awake, and the moonlight moved across the wall, he used to wonder. Once free, he would love to see them again, if they were still alive, and always supposing they still wanted to see him.

When his time was up he found a job in the town but he could not settle. Something seemed to be drawing him home, with an urge he could not get away from. Every time he went for a walk something reminded him of the small brick house - a clump of pansies, a child on a swing , a little boy running home from school.

He did not want to arrive penniless, and he walked or hitched a good deal of the long journey home. He could have arrived earlier, but twenty miles away he was suddenly overcome with misgivings. What right had he to walk in like this? Could they ever reconcile the haggard man he had become with the boy they had loved and who had so bitterly disappointed them?

He bought some food and spent most of that day sitting under a tree. The letter he posted that evening was quite short, but it had taken him hours to write. It ended with these words - 'I know it is unreasonable of me to suppose that you want to see me,.. so it's up to you. I'll come to the end of the road early Thursday morning. If you want me home, hang a white handkerchief in the window of my old bedroom. If it's there I'll come; if not, I'll wave goodbye to the old house and go on my way.'

And now it was Thursday morning. He had arrived at the end of the street. It was still there! But having got there, he felt in no hurry at all. He just sat down on the pavement and stared at the stones.

Well, he could not put it off forever, and after all they might have moved. If the handkerchief was not there he would make a few enquiries before leaving the town. He had not yet had the courage to face what he would do if they were there and simply did not want him.

16

He got up painfully, for he was stiff from sleeping out, and the street was still in shadow. Shivering a little, he walked slowly towards the old plane tree where he knew he could see the old house as clear as clear. He would not look till he got there.

He stood under the boughs with his eyes shut for a moment. Then he drew a long breath and looked. Then he stood staring and staring.

The sun was already shining on the little red brick house, but it no longer seemed to be a little red brick house for every wall was festooned with white. Every window was hung with sheets, pillowcases, towels, tablecloths, handkerchiefs and table napkins; and white muslin curtains trailed across the roof from the attic window. It looked like a snow house gleaming in the morning light.

His parents were taking no risks. The man threw back his head and gave a cry of relief. Then he ran up the street and straight in at the open front door.

Keynote: As kind as a father is to his children, so kind is the Lord to those who honour him. Psalm 103:13
Let the wicked leave their way of life and change their way of thinking. Let them turn to the Lord, our God; he is merciful and quick to forgive. Isaiah 55:7

Prayer: Thank you Father, that you love me more dearly than any earthly father, for all love flows from you. Your love never forgets me, even when I forget you. You always welcome me back even when I have sinned. You love to forgive me even when I don't deserve it. Thank you for your everlasting love.

Think: Can you say for yourself that God loves you? In what ways are you aware of his love?

...Who made me and bought me back...
Genesis 1:26–31 and 3

2. THE LOST BOAT

John had spent many Saturday afternoons in the garage, building that boat. He had carved the hulk out of a solid block of wood, chiselling it out and sand papering it. His mother had helped with the sails but he had a model and knew exactly what to do about the rigging. It was a beautiful model sailing ship, and the best of it was that he had made it all himself.

Now it was finished, and it sat in state in the living room, admired by all. His father was especially impressed. 'I am proud of you for being so clever with your hands, John,' he said. 'What are you going to make next?'

But John had not thought about what next. His boat was enough for the present.

It was a lovely spring day when he took the boat to the canal to sail it, and he headed for the best place - a little sandy beach, hidden by rushes where he had once found a moorhen's nest. It was perfect sailing weather, sunny and windy, and as he launched his boat, the breeze caught its sails and bore it out into the amber water of the current. He squatted at the edge and gave play to the string. In a few minutes he would climb the bank and run along the towpath, but first he would just stay there to admire its beauty. So absorbed was he, that he never heard voices just behind him, and he jumped when three boys a good deal older than himself slid down into the rushes and squatted beside him. He clutched the string tightly, for these were not boys he knew. He thought they probably came from one of the barges that travelled up and down the canal.

'Here, give us a go,' said the oldest.

'Well, only for a minute,' said John. 'I'm just going to pull her in.'

He felt nervous and alone, for these boys looked thoroughly rough types. The biggest lad had already snatched the string from his hand, and was hauling in the boat, pulling it over on its side and drenching the sails. As it approached the bank John found himself suddenly tipped into a bed of nettles and rushes. His hands squelched in the soft mud and dirt flew into his eyes blinding him for a moment. When at last he struggled to his feet, spitting out moss and mud, there was neither boy nor boat to be seen - only the trampled reeds and the weeping willows.

He scrambled up the bank but the boys had disappeared behind the hedges, and he could not even see in what direction they had gone. Besides, if he did catch them, there was nothing he could do against the three of them, so he wiped his hands and turned home. He knew that his parents had gone out to tea, and he doubted whether the police would be very impressed if he phoned up and told them.

When his parents returned, his father set out at once to make enquiries, but no-one in the locality had seen three strange boys. John was very quiet at suppertime, and when he was alone in bed he found himself crying. His father had offered to help him make another one, but it would not be the same. This was his first, his very own. He would never forget it.

The weeks passed and John and his father made another boat and sailed it in the river, but John did not forget the first one. Sometimes he would lie awake and remember the shine of the paint and the billowing of the sails, and wonder where it had got to.

One afternoon he cycled into town to buy a birthday present for his mother, and having found what he wanted he took a short-cut home through the narrow back streets. He loved the pokey little second-hand junk shops, and dawdled along gazing in at the windows. Suddenly he stopped dead; for there in the centre of a shop window, along with an old guitar and brass coal scuttle, stood his boat.

Propping his bicycle against a wall, he burst into the shop.

'That boat in the window,' he gasped. 'It's mine! I made it.'

The little old shopkeeper looked at him over his spectacles.

'On the contrary, young man,' he replied, 'it's mine! I bought it from a couple of boys weeks ago. I've just put it in the window.'

'But I made it. It's mine, truly it is. Please give it to me.'

'Not unless you pay the proper price. It's marked on the ticket.'

'But I've spent all my money.'

'Then you must get some more.'

John realised that argument was hopeless, but there was still time. He sped home; his father was gardening.

'Dad,' he shouted breathlessly, 'can you lend me £4?'

'Why?' asked his father cautiously, 'How will you repay it?'

'I'll clean the car, or mow the lawn, or do anything you want, but I must have it. It's my boat .... if I hurry, I can get back before the shop closes.'

His father looked longingly at his roses, sighed and nodded towards the car.

'Hop in,' he said, 'it's nearly closing time. You'd never get it home on the bike without messing up the rigging.'

The old man was just about to put up the shutters when John rushed in.

'I've got it,' he shouted. 'Now please give me my boat!'

'I'll sell you my boat,' said the old man with a chuckle, handing it over.

They drove home in silence, John examining his treasure. Only as they reached the gate did he speak.

'You know what, Dad?' he said. 'I was thinking, this boat belongs to me twice. I made it and I bought it. Isn't that amazing?'

'Very,' agreed his father, 'and all the more reason to look after it...'

But John was not listening. He had shot off to show the miracle to his mother.

Author's Note: *So God created us for himself, but we strayed away and began to live selfishly, preferring to please ourselves. Sin, rejection of God, put us under the power of the devil. But God himself came to us in Jesus Christ, the God man, and paid the penalty for all our sins with his own life. God redeemed us and can therefore now claim us as twice his own.*

Keynote: The word 'redeem' means to buy back something that belonged to you. Isaiah 43:1 says, 'The Lord who created you says, 'Do not be afraid - I have saved (redeemed) you. I have called you by my name - you are mine.'

Prayer: O God, my Father and Creator, thank you that you created me for yourself and loved me even before I was born. Thank you for coming to me in Jesus, and paying the price of sin, when Jesus died. Help me to give myself to you as twice yours because you made me, and because you have redeemed me.

Think: Why do you think God still cares about people, even after thousands of years when they have been turning their back on him? What has kept God from saying, 'If people choose to go their own way rather than my way, I'll just leave them to it'?

... Who removed the wall between us and him
Ephesians 2: 12,18

3. THE CLOSED WINDOW

Anna had never really been ill in her life, except for a cold, and she could not imagine why her throat was so sore, and why she felt so miserable. Her mother stared at her when she pushed away her sausage and baked beans.

'I thought it was your favourite supper,' she said. 'Whatever is the matter with you, Anna?'

'Nothing,' whispered Anna, and then everything seemed to spin round and she laid her head on the table.

'You're ill, Anna!' Mummy's frightened voice sounded far away. 'Let me feel your forehead! Why, bless the child, she's burning hot! Up to bed with you, love!'

It was a strange night. Anna woke and slept and burned and shivered; every time she dozed she had queer frightening dreams and called out for her mother, who was always there. When the darkness paled, and the birds began to twitter, Anna woke up properly and wanted to know what was happening to her.

'You've got a nasty sore throat and fever,' said her mother, who looked as though she had not slept all night. 'Daddy's just going to phone the doctor.'

The doctor came quite quickly and swabbed her throat and examined her all over. He looked rather grave and Anna could hear him talking to her mother in the passage, but she could not hear what they said.

Hours passed, and Anna dozed and woke and sipped water, and her mother sat beside her. Then she fell into a deep sleep and it was night again, and mother lay on a mattress on the floor. 'As long as she is there,' thought Anna, 'everything is all right. But I do wish this sore throat would go.'

But next morning the phone rang and her father came up to give the message. The swab showed that Anna had diphtheria (an infectious fever now virtually belonging to the past). She must therefore get herself ready to go into the Fever Hospital. The ambulance would call for her in about half an hour.

'You'll come too, won't you, Mummy?' croaked Anna, fixing her eyes on her mother. Her mother hesitated and looked very distressed. 'I'm afraid they won't allow that,' she said. 'They are taking you away because you are infectious. But I'm sure the nurses will be very kind, and I will come this afternoon.'

If Anna had been feeling well she might have enjoyed hospital, for there were other children in the ward and the nurses were kind. But her throat still hurt badly and she felt terribly homesick, so she just lay there, fighting back the tears and watching the door. Her mother had said she would come that afternoon and Anna wanted her more than anything else in the world.

Then suddenly the nurse came over to her and said, 'Look Anna, there's your mother at the window. Don't sit up now! Just wave and give her a nice smile.'

'But,' cried Anna, 'tell her where the door is. Please let her come in quick. I want to tell her something ... it's very important.'

'I'm sorry,' said the nurse very gently, 'but no-one is allowed in, because all the children here are infectious. You don't want your mother to get ill, do you? If you've got a message, I'll give it to her.'

Anna shook her head. She had no message, and was too disappointed to speak. Her strong, comforting mother was there, longing to come to her, the only person who could put things right, but all they could do was to look at each other helplessly through the glass. Nurse would not even open the window. They smiled bravely again to cheer each other up, and then waved goodbye. And Anna, who was feeling very ill, buried her face in the pillow and wept, because it was just as though her mother had never been.

Time passed slowly and Anna got better every day, and then a wonderful thing happened. Anna was sitting by the window in her dressing-gown, and her mother appeared as usual. But that afternoon the nurse opened the window wide.

'Now you can both have a nice talk,' she said.

And how they talked! There was so much to tell and hear - a whole week's news. They talked and talked until the sun disappeared behind the trees and nurse told Anna to go back to bed. And how deeply and sweetly she slept that night, knowing that there would never be anything between herself and her mother again. Every day now the window would be open.

Now time moved faster, for the weather was fine, and Anna was allowed to walk with her mother in the garden and to play outside with other children. She could look through the railings and see the blossom in the hedges and the new lambs skipping, and she knew it would not be long now before she went home. And sure enough the day came. She was drinking cocoa at the ward table, when the doctor came in with a paper in his hand.

'Well Anna,' he said, 'you seem all clear. Phone her mother, please Nurse. Anna can go home today.'

So that afternoon, instead of saying goodbye at the gate, Anna got into the car and they drove away together. No more windows, no more goodbyes! Anna was going home.

Author's Note: *God is the source of all life, love, comfort and happiness. Whatever we may think, we shall never find real, lasting joy apart from him. But sin has made a barrier between us. I cannot come to God until the barrier of sin has been taken away. God has come to me in Jesus, and by his death, he has pulled down that wall. The New Testament says that Jesus took the barrier out of the way and nailed it* *to the cross. There is therefore an open way to God, and an open way to heaven, for all who are willing to believe that Jesus is that Way.*

Keynote: Your presence fills me with joy and brings me pleasure forever. Psalm 16:11 It is because of your sins that he doesn't hear you. It is your sins that separate you from God when you try to worship him. Isaiah 59:2

Prayer: God, I know you are the only one who can make me happy. My sin made a barrier between us but Jesus bore it away. Help me to understand that, if I trust him, there is nothing between me and you. I can come to you at any moment of the day or night. Thank you that you are preparing a home for us in heaven. Cleanse me, and make me ready for when you shall call me.

Think: Why did it cost God so much to remove that barrier of sin - the death of his Son? Why wasn't it possible for God to turn a blind eye on human sin in order to spare the Son he loved so much?

I BELIEVE IN GOD'S SON JESUS CHRIST

4. WHY SHEIKH ALI RAN

Ali, the Arab Sheikh, sat at his table in his rich apartment. It was a beautiful room looking down on a garden where irises and narcissi grew in the shade of a great twisted mulberry tree. The Sheikh was master of a large estate, and his ledgers and account books lay spread out in front of him, and his secretary was hard at work.

Sometimes he concentrated on his books but sometimes his gaze strayed out of the window to where a little boy climbed on the great, gnarled boughs of the mulberry tree. Black-eyed, black haired, dressed in jeans, he looked like any other boy; but this was Sadik, the only son and heir and the light of his father's eyes, who was playing down below, and that was why the accounts seemed to be moving rather slowly that morning.

Sheikh Ali turned the pages of his diary thoughtfully. Important guests were coming that night and his wife had gone home to a family wedding. Well, no matter! He had plenty of excellent servants. He pressed the electric bell, and the messenger glided in noiselessly.

'Fetch Abdullah and the cook,' said the master. A moment later they stood before him in their spotless uniforms. Abdullah was to go to market and buy all that was necessary. He bowed and withdrew. The cook was to bake and roast and serve up a sumptuous banquet. She inclined her head and left the room.

'Fetch the gardener,' ordered the master, and in he came. He was to pick the choicest fruit and flowers, and he smiled and went away. He loved displaying the harvest of his beautiful garden and orchard.

There were letters to deliver and interviews to arrange.

A wall was crumbling near the sheepfolds and the foreman was consulted. A dozen matters needed attending to, and a dozen servants went quietly off in different directions. The master sipped his black coffee and never moved from his desk. He had no need to move from his desk, only to give orders.

Suddenly there was a loud cry from the garden. The master leaped up and ran to the window. His son had fallen out of the tree with a scream. He lay in a bed of irises, holding up his arms, crying for help. His father did not ring the bell, or send for a servant. He ran down the stairs and past the porter who stood staring at the master as he charged down the path.

'I'm coming my son, ' he cried, and stooping down, he lifted the bruised child in his arms, carefully supporting the twisted ankle. Holding the little boy tight against his expensive suit, he carried him past the porter, past the secretary, and into his own bedroom.

Author's Note: *God, our Creator, Father, Redeemer and the Source of all life and love, has many servants to do his will. But when God heard the cry of his children who had spoiled their lives with sin, he sent neither angel or prophet, he came himself. He clothed himself in a human body, and came to us in Jesus, the Son of God. Paul said, 'God, in Christ, was reconciling the world to himself.' Jesus said, 'Whoever has seen me has seen the Father.'*

Keynote: Praise the Lord, you strong and mighty angels, who obey his commandments ... praise the Lord ... you servants of his, who do his will! Psalm 103:20,21

Lightning and hail, snow and clouds, strong winds that obey his command... praise him. Psalm 148:8

In the past, God spoke to our ancestors many times and in many ways through the prophets. Hebrews 1:1

Prayer: O God, my Father and Creator, I want to think

about your greatness. You are the Lord of the universe and the galaxies and outer space. Your angels and messengers obey your commands all the time. I thank you that when I sinned and spoiled the life you gave me, you came yourself in Jesus. You loved me and came - became a child like me, to get near to me and lead me to God. Teach me to love Jesus, for in Him I shall find God.

Think: In your opinion, what does the fact that God came HIMSELF, in his Son, tell us about his character?

5. THE UNRECOGNISED GUEST

The time in English history when England was invaded by the fierce, seafaring nation called the Danes was a terrifying period. They came in terrible ships with dragons' heads on the prow, and they wore steel helmets. Wherever they went they plundered and murdered and burnt houses and churches, and the English fled from them, until a brave king called Alfred made a stand against them on sea and land. At first he was successful, but at one point he too was driven back. So fierce and strong was the onslaught of his enemies that he had to flee from his palace and hide in the forest disguised as a vagabond. A great price was set on his head by the Danish king, and he dared not reveal his identity except to a few faithful followers.

One was a herdsman called Ulfric, who loved his king and would never betray him. Ulfric begged the king to take shelter in his cottage, but he did not trust his wife who was rather talkative, so he did not tell her who the visitor was.

Alfred was very sad and would sit for hours thinking of his lost kingdom and trying to work out new military tactics. But the herdsman's wife had no use for a strong man who sat brooding. When he spoke she had no idea that she was listening to her king. There was plenty of work to be done, and she could not understand why her husband should tolerate such an idle vagabond. So she waited until Ulfric had gone to the fields and then started on the stranger.

'Now come along, good man,' she said. 'There's no need to sit idle. You don't seem good for much, but you can watch these cakes on the grid while I go to the well. As soon as they begin to brown, turn them over, and when they are brown right through, take them off.'

Alfred sat by the fire deep in thought. Perhaps he saw visions of victory in the glowing wood. If only he could rally his forces ... meet and defeat the enemy ... if only he could meet up with his captains.

He was startled by a box on the ear and an angry torrent of abuse. He woke from his dreams of battle and victory to a smell of burning. The cakes were as black as cinders, and the herdsman's wife was very, very angry.

'You lazy good-for-nothing,' she shouted, 'can't I even trust you ...'

'Hush, hush woman!' It was the scandalised voice of Ulfric who had just come in. Seeing that she had no intention of hushing, he added desperately,

'Hold your tongue. Do you not know your king?'

We do not know what happened next, but we know Alfred was a gentle, just man, and was probably very sorry for his carelessness. We know too, that in the end he gathered his loyal men and they met and defeated the enemy, and Alfred went back to his palace and ruled for years over his kingdom, a loved and honoured king. But he never forgot the kindness of Ulfric, and he took him from the herds and made him a Bishop. So his wife must often have curtseyed to the king she failed to recognise when he came to her in disguise.

Keynote: The Word was in the world, and though God made the world through him, yet the world did not recognise him. He came to his own country, but his people did not receive him. John 1:10,11

Very few recognised God in the disguise of a baby. The innkeeper shut the door on him. Later, his brothers and neighbours thought he was an ordinary child. When he did miracles they thought he was just a good man. But a few recognised him as God - the shepherds and wise men; Simeon and Anna; his parents, and later his disciples and a few people whom he healed or talked to, and the Roman soldier at the Cross.

Prayer: O God, my Father and Creator, help me to recognise you in Jesus. Help me, as I read the gospels, to see your glory in Jesus. Teach me to hear the voice of God as I read the words of Jesus.

Think: God didn't come in the way most men would expect - in glorious splendid clothes, like a king. How would you have expected him to come? Do you think that still now, God comes to you in different ways and you fail to recognise him?

6. FOOTSTEPS IN THE SNOW

Janet was thrilled with their new home in the country. They first went to visit it in April, and while her father and her brother Martin explored the garage and tool-shed, and her mother toured the house, Janet ran out into the garden. Beyond the lawn the garden sloped to a rockery and beyond that was an orchard of apple trees in blossom and long deep grass where cowslips grew. And it was there, lying in the grass and looking up into the blossom that the family found her twenty minutes later. Her mother laughed.

'Aren't you interested in the house, Jan?' she asked. 'You can't live in the orchard, you know!' 'Yes I am,' said Janet. 'Can I please have the bedroom that looks out on the orchard?' And can I have that funny little attic for a workshop?' said Martin. 'And can I have the bottom of the orchard for my hens?' asked Dad.

Everyone got what they wanted. The hens were white leghorns and the children never got tired of collecting the eggs. Their father had to leave for work quite early and did not get home till six, so Martin took the hens their breakfast before he went to school, and Janet gave them their supper when she came home from school. She loved wandering through the long grass and clover and sorrel in the orchard, and waiting till the birds had all crowded to her feet.

'In the spring they'll have chicks,' she thought to herself joyfully, 'and I shall watch them hatch.'

Autumn came and the apples ripened. The children picked pounds of blackberries. The woods beyond the garden blazed red and russet and gold, and the swallows flew away. Then the leaves began to fall, and they lit the wood fires in the evening; and one night, while they slept, it started to snow.

It snowed hard and unceasingly for three nights and two days, and the whole countryside was covered. The hens huddled in their coops fussing and clucking, and the robins came to the windowsill. On the third morning Dad got up early, swept the path to the gate, and they walked to school in the car ruts. Tomorrow would be Saturday and they would go tobogganing.

Janet came out of school at four, and walked home alone as Martin had gone off with a friend. She loved the silent countryside, the imprint of tiny claws in the snow and, where the wood came down to the road, the tracks of little cloven footprints. There was a yellow light in the west, and strange blue shadows on the fields. The house was silent too, for Mother had gone out.

She changed quickly, put on her Wellington boots and made up the mash for the hens. How cold and bored they must be, she thought as she hurried towards the lawn. Then she stopped and gave a little gasp. How could she ever get across? She was small and light for her age, and snow lay thick and unbroken, much deeper than the height of her boots.

The sun was already setting and it would be dark when Martin got home. She had better think of some way.

She stared at the lawn. Was it just shadows, or were there slight marks in the snow? She could not quite tell in the twilight. Then she remembered. Martin had given the hens their breakfast; he must have crossed the lawn that morning. Of course it was many hours back and a further light fall had obliterated his tracks, but at least she could try. She set her foot carefully on the first mark and it sank in only a little on to hard trodden snow. If she could reach the next one and the next, she could get there safely.

It was very difficult, for Martin had long legs and enormous feet, but somehow she managed, balancing, stretching and putting her small foot into the print ahead, right on through the orchard where it was easier because she could cling to the apple boughs. The hens were delighted to see her and gave her a noisy welcome, and she cleared a patch for them to come out and gobble their food. It had stopped snowing and she stayed with them till they had all hurried back into the coop. She rather liked their squawking in the vast, awesome silence of the snow.

The journey back was easier because the track was more obvious, but her feet were bitterly cold and the world looked strange and grey. As she came out from the orchard a broad beam of light shone out from the kitchen window and she knew her mother was home. She felt very glad indeed. It would be good to take off these boots and have some hot tea, and tell her mother all about her adventure.

The footsteps led her right to the door, and she almost fell through the door into the warmth and light.

'Is that you, Jan?' called her mother's voice. 'Shut the door quickly! Isn't it cold? Let's make some toast, and have tea together by the fire.'

Keynote: For Christ himself suffered for you and left you an example, so that you would follow in his steps. 1 Peter 2:21

Prayer: O God, as I read the Gospels, I see the footprints of Jesus, like a shining track of obedience, love, truth, and courage. Help me to follow his example. I know I often go my own way, but help me today to be a true follower of Jesus, living and speaking as he did, when he was my age. Lead me, in the end, to your Home in heaven.

Think: Why did Jesus live for thirty-three years on this earth? Why did he become a child, a boy in a carpenter's shop, a man who travelled about and was tired and hungry and homeless? What is the most important point in Jesus's example? How can you best follow this in your own life?

7. THE MAN WHO WAS DIFFERENT

Many years ago, before China was a Communist state, two young men set out early in the morning along a rough country track. On their backs were rucksacks filled with Bibles, New Testaments and Gospels, for they were going to a little market town to sell their books, and, if possible, to talk to the country people, who worshipped idols, about the living God.

They swung along happily between deep green rice fields, and after about two hours they reached the outskirts of the market town - an open space filled with people, mules and wares. The young men hesitated.

'They may never have seen anyone like us,' said the younger, whose name was James.

'No, but we will show them the books,' said David, the elder of the two. 'Come on, I think they have seen us.'

He was right. As they approached, all faces seemed turned towards them, and they were surrounded by a curious crowd. Some laughed, some questioned, but no one seemed hostile, and the books were eagerly bought, for, although most of the farmers could not read, many had relatives or children who could, and a book was a rare and precious object - and so cheap!

David and James moved slowly through the market. It was a sordid place. The beggars whined for coins and the merchants thrust them aside. Everyone was bargaining, quarrelling, cheating or trying to get the better of someone else. The young men made for a clump of trees and squatted down among a crowd of people who were eating their midday meal in the shade, and pulled out their remaining books.

'Tells us about them,' said a farmer lazily. 'We can not read.'

What could David tell? What would they understand about a living, loving God? Would they care? He looked round on the upturned faces, some dull, some greedy and cunning, and he began to speak about Jesus, the one who went about doing good.

'He taught people to love their enemies, and said, "Blessed are the peacemakers and the merciful, and the pure in heart."' The people listened in amazement, and others gathered. Warming to his subject, David went on and on...

Suddenly he was interrupted. A man pushed through the crowd smiling:

'I know that man,' he announced. 'He lives in our village. Come I will take you to him.'

In vain David explained that the man of whom he was speaking had long left this earth. The man brushed aside his explanations. 'No, no,' he said, 'this friend of yours, there is only one like him. He will be glad to see you, since you know him so well. Come, follow me. He lives in the next valley.'

David and James were quite ready to follow; the man's words had stirred their curiosity and there was still plenty of time. The farmer was in a hurry to start, so they shouldered their rucksacks and followed him, eating their lunch as they walked. An hour's walking brought them to the village - an open space scattered with tumbledown huts, where pigs rooted in the dust, and rubbish decayed by the side of the track.

'Your friend lives here,' said the farmer, pushing a child with swollen infected eyes out of the way. 'He will be surprised to see you.'

Even before the farmer stopped, David and James knew that they had arrived. There was no rubbish in front of this hut, and instead of trampled mud, green things grew. It was different. The man at the door was different too. His face wasn't greedy or cunning but kind and simple. The child with the infected eyes crept softly to the door and was not pushed away.

'Your friends,' said the farmer. 'They talked of you in the market. I guided them.' James handed over a coin and the farmer went off. They were left with this gentle stranger.

'Come in,' said the man courteously, 'and be seated. You have walked far, and I have little to offer. I will make tea.' While they drank they talked. 'What are you doing in this out-of-the-way village?'

'We are selling books.'

'What are your books about?'

'About God the Creator and his son Jesus Christ.'

'Jesus?'

The man rose up with a strange brightness on his face.

'Could it be the same? Do you know him?' he breathed. 'Could it be the man I know?'

He went to a box and came back with an old tattered Gospel of Mark in his hand.

'This is the book that tells about my Jesus,' he said, and he seemed to linger lovingly over the name. 'Years ago a man sold it to me in the market, and I read it day and night. Never had I known a man like that! I said, 'He is so good, will I become like him?' Each day I ask myself, what would he do if he were here in my house? Sometimes I think he really is here in this hut, or ploughing or harvesting with me, or walking the road to the market. Could it be the same Jesus that you know?'

They stared at him, his face so bright, so beaming with love.

'Yes it's the same Jesus,' said James. 'There is only one Jesus.'

'Was I right?' asked the farmer loudly, suddenly sticking his head through the door. 'Was this the man you were talking about?'

'The man we were talking about is here with us,' said David. 'He lives in this house. You were perfectly right.'

Author's Note: *Have you been to a buttercup field before sunrise, and seen every flower closed? A few hours later each flower will be open and reflecting the sun. Not by struggling or by working, but simply looking up at the light. So as we look at the perfect, loving life of Jesus in the Gospels and seek to be like him, we shall gradually be changed.*

Keynote: All of us, then, reflect the glory of the Lord with uncovered faces; and that same glory, coming from the Lord... transforms us into his likeness in an ever greater degree of glory. 2 Corinthians 3:18

Prayer: Lord, as I read about Jesus in the Gospels, and think about him and try to be like him please change me to be like him.

Think: Carefully make a list of seven simple, practical ways in which you know you can follow Jesus and show your family that you love them. Concentrate on these ways, starting with one and adding one a day. Once you have struggled through your first week, try to keep going until you can see that your life has been changed.

8. THE RING AND THE ROSES

When Francis was born, no one suspected that there was anything the matter with him. He was just another beautiful baby. Not till he was several months old, did his parents begin to wonder and fear.

Why did he never turn his head when they came into the room?

Why did he never start when his older sister slammed the door?

Why did his rattle seem to never give him any pleasure?

At last they took him to a doctor and were not really surprised when he broke the bad news to them. 'Francis is completely deaf, and will probably never speak either.'

At first his parents were heartbroken, but as time passed, it seemed impossible to feel sad in the presence of young Francis. He was so happy, so intelligent, so eager to discover the world of sight. He learned to understand them by lip-reading and sign language, and they, too understood his gestures and strange noises.

They sent him to a special school for deaf children, and there he discovered all sorts of ways of communicating. And his mother would watch him and think, 'How can I be sad? No one could have a better, brighter happier boy than mine!'

Francis loved birds and flowers, and would wander for hours in the fields and woods, but no one taught him about God the Creator until his uncle came to stay and brought a picture book of Bible stories. Francis and his uncle understood each other quickly, and night after night they would sit together, and by pictures and signs and lip-reading,

Francis learned how God had come down to us in Jesus, and how, through knowing Jesus, he could know God. He had always wondered who made the seeds grow, and guided the swallows when they flew away, so he was glad to learn about God.

They had looked at most of the pictures and Francis was beginning to know a good deal about the love and goodness of Jesus. But one night his uncle turned the page and Francis saw a picture of Jesus hanging on a cross between two other men, and a great crowd of people gathered in front of him.

Francis could not understand it and he wanted to cry with anger and disappointment. But somehow, by means of a white paper heart and a black paper heart his uncle tried to make him understand that Jesus, whose heart was pure and sinless, was dying for the sins of all the other people whose hearts were sinful.

But even after seeing the picture many times, there were things that Francis could not understand. He knew that one man could die instead of another, and he pointed to Christ and the dying thief, and nodded. But how could one man die for so many - all the crowd at the cross, the people in the street below? He pointed to the many figures in the picture and shook his head.

His uncle thought for a while. Then he drew his gold wedding ring off his finger and laid it on the table. Then he went into the garden, where the late roses were still in bloom ad gathered a bunch of withered flowers, their petals spoiled and ready to fall. He sat down at the table and laid a petal beside the ring.

'Which would you choose?' he signed.

Francis pointed to the gold ring.

His uncle shook about ten petals onto the table and gathered them into a heap.

'Which would you choose?' he signed again.

Again Francis pointed to the gold ring.

Uncle went on and on, shaking the spoiled dying petals on the table and gathering them in a great heap before the shining ring. But even when there were over a hundred, Francis, without the least hesitation, pointed to the ring.

Suddenly he understood and signed to his uncle to stop. He pushed away the petals and laid the ring carefully on the cross; then he scattered a few petals on the crowd. He knew now that if his uncle was to pick and scatter every rose in the world, the ring would always be worth far more than a mountain of spoiled petals. And he knew too that the shining, sinless life of a man hanging on the cross was precious enough to pay for the sins of all the spoiled sinful men and women and children in the world. With a bright smile Francis laid his hand on the gold ring.

Keynote: Everyone must die once, and after that be judged by God. In the same manner Christ also was offered in sacrifice once to take away the sins of many. Hebrews 9:27,28

Prayer: Thank you Lord that your life was perfect and sinless, and when you offered yourself instead of sinners, it was a perfect offering. Thank you that you offered up your love for my selfishness, and your goodness for my sinfulness. Help me to understand the meaning of your death. Help me to love you, because you loved me so much.

Think: What does the death of Jesus mean to you?

WHO DIED ON
THE CROSS
TO SAVE THE
WORLD AND ME

Jesus died to save me from eternal death

Romans 5:6–9

9. THE SAFE PLACE

The farm lay blazing in the midsummer heat; the harvest was in and the corn stacked, and it would soon be time for fruit picking.

The farmer leaned on the gate and gazed at the stubble fields. It had been a good crop, and he had done well on the poultry too.

Bill, the farm-hand was also having a rest under the haystack. He had finished his lunch and his mug of ale and was smoking a cigarette. There was half an hour to go, and it was pleasant in the shade of the rick. A warm smell of herbs came from the farm garden; it made Bill feel drowsy ... he closed his eyes. Bill was asleep.

He woke suddenly, only a few minutes later, and wondered where the loud crackling noise came from. Then he smelt the smoke and leaped to his feet with a cry of horror.

The cigarette stump had rolled into the burnt grass, but it had done its deadly work. Already the rick was ablaze and the flames blowing toward the hen-coops and the house.

Bill ran as he had never run before. The farmer would be at his dinner and they must phone the fire brigade.

Nothing could be done about the rick. It had already turned from a smouldering heap to a leaping furnace of flame: but they might save the poultry and the house. He burst into the house like a madman, and dialled 999.

'Come quick,' he urged. 'It's on the main road - two and a half miles out.' He flung down the receiver, and found the farmer, pale-faced at his elbow. 'The barn's caught,' he said shortly, 'so now it's the poultry and the house. Open the three gates into the meadow and shoo all the poultry towards them - they'll find their way; and I'll get the hose onto the coops and the wall of the house.'

Together they fought the flames till their faces were black and their eyebrows singed. The farmer's wife had taken their children to the far end of the paddock and was hurriedly carrying out their most precious possessions in armfuls. She was the first to hear the clanging of the fire bell and to see the engine sweep into the yard.

It took some time to get the flames under control. The rick and the barn burned down into a sodden mass of ashes, but the hencoops, the house and the stable were saved. The wife carried her baby and all her most precious possessions back into the house, and made cups of tea for the weary firemen. Bill slunk off home before anyone got round to asking how the fire started.

The farmer went out to the coops and put down the chicken feed, and the poultry came wandering back, squawking and suspicious. He counted them carefully; one family was missing, the white hen and her chickens.

Where could they have got to? The chickens were very young - nine little fluffy balls of yellow down. But he had seen them running after the hen towards the safety of the open field, and she was an excellent mother. He would go and have a look around.

There were three openings in the stone wall leading out to the fields and the farmer went out at the main gate and walked slowly, examining the ditches. Finding nothing, he made for the small stile nearest the blazing barn, and here he stopped short, and stood staring at the ground. The hen sat in a heap in the gap, her head hanging over on one side, her feathers scorched and discoloured by smoke. She was quite dead, and yet the path to safety lay in front of her and the way was open. Why had she sat down and died like that?

The farmer stooped and picked her up, and out from under her limp wings ran the nine fluffy chickens, alive and cheeping. The farmer gathered them into a box and put them by the kitchen stove cuddled up in a piece of blanket. The seven-year-old just could not get over it.

'She could easily have saved herself, couldn't she, Daddy?' she kept saying, 'but I suppose they were too small to run fast .. perhaps they couldn't see the way in the smoke .. perhaps they were going the wrong way. Anyhow, she knew the safest place was under her wings, didn't she, Daddy? .. I suppose she just sat down and called them to come, and died instead of them. Wasn't she a good mother, Daddy!'

'I shan't have much time to be a good mother if I've got to bring that lot up by hand,' grumbled the farmer's wife. 'As though I hadn't enough to do already!'

But the seven-year-old laid her curly head against the blanket and whispered, 'The gate was open. The hen could have saved herself; but she might have left her little ones behind, lost in the smoke. Little chickens, little chickens, I'm so glad you came when your mummy called you, or you'd all be dead. Little chickens, I'll be your mummy instead.'

Author's Note: *Jesus was sinless. He could have gone back to heaven without dying; but he would have gone alone. We would have remained cut off from God because of our sins, and this finally leads to real, eternal death. So Jesus chose to die instead of us, so that we can come to him and live.*

Keynote: This is how we know what love is: Christ gave his life for us. 1 John 3:16

I live by faith in the Son of God who loved me and gave his life for me. Galatians 2:20

Prayer: Lord, I understand that you loved me enough to die for me, that I might have eternal life, and you will call me to come and shelter in Jesus from sin and eternal death. Teach me to answer your call. Thank you for loving me; thank you for dying for me.

Think: Jesus allowed others to torture him to death for our (your) sake. Can his love still be doubted? Do you think this can help you sometimes also to bear the suffering for others?

10. THE FORBIDDEN PATH

Joy lived in North London, so it was quite exciting when her mother announced one day at breakfast, 'Miss Fairfax, an old friend of mine, has moved to a cottage in Epping Forest. She wants us both to go and have tea with her on Saturday. She has got a lovely garden, so you can explore while we have a chat.'

Saturday dawned clear and sunny and Joy and her mother set out in the car after lunch. Soon they left the suburbs behind them, and found themselves driving through tunnels of beech trees. Joy stuck her head far out of the window and sniffed.

'Oh Mum,' said Joy, 'I wish we lived in the country!'

'Perhaps we shall one day,' said her mother 'when Dad gets his promotion. I should love it too. Look, there's the cottage.'

Joy greeted her hostess politely, but hardly noticed what she looked like, for her whole attention was focused on the garden. It was a mass of summer flowers and led to a shining meadow of ragwort, with a pond shaded by weeping willows. Her mother laughed.

'Joy will wake up soon,' she said. 'She seldom gets into real proper country like this. Can she explore round till teatime?'

'Of course,' said Miss Fairfax, 'go where you like ..except don't go up that path between the laurel hedges, because ... oh, here comes Trixie! Down Trixie! Don't get so excited! She's a good friendly dog, but she will jump up on visitors; Trixie will love to go for a walk with you Joy, and we'll ring the bell out of the window when tea's ready, so you can hear it in the meadow.'

Miss Fairfax and Joy's mother disappeared into the house, and Joy and Trixie made for the pond. They spent a happy, muddy half hour exploring, and then they wandered back to the garden. Joy stared thoughtfully at the path that curved away round the laurel bushes. She thought it led to an apple orchard, for she could see some boughs against the skyline.

'I wonder why she didn't want me to go down there,' thought Joy. 'Did she think I'd eat her apples? Well, I won't .. but I do wonder!'

She walked round the rockery, but it only brought her back to the same place.

'I really would like to know,' thought Joy. 'Perhaps it's some secret, or some special animal .. I'll just go as far as the curve and peep round. There's nothing as far as that, anyhow!'

She tiptoed down the path. Trixie growled.

She peered round the corner; there was nothing mysterious to be seen. It led, as she thought, to a small apple orchard. Whatever could be dangerous or secret about an orchard? She would just tiptoe to the edge of the trees and then run back.

Trixie growled again, but she took no notice.

'There's nothing here at all,' thought Joy, standing under the first tree and looking up. 'It's a nice place, I wonder ... OH HELP!'

She had not noticed the swarm of bees on the apple tree. Her curls were nearly touching them, and they suddenly rose up in an angry black cloud, buzzing angrily. Joy screamed and ran, the bees behind her, and it was really Trixie that saved the situation. The collie ran backwards behind her, barking furiously, and the bees drew back. Only one, flying high, pursued her as she rushed through the laurel bushes and burst out onto the lawn.

Miss Fairfax and her mother heard her scream and ran to the window.

'Horrors!' said Miss Fairfax. 'It's the bees! I told her not to ..'

But her mother did not wait to hear what Miss Fairfax had told Joy. She ran into the garden towards the terrified little girl, with the great big bee buzzing round her head.

'Get behind me, Joy,' she shouted. 'Quick! Hide!'

Joy darted behind her mother, and the bee, alighting on the bare outstretched arm gave mother a good sting. It then flew over her shoulder and continued to buzz round Joy.

'He's after me!' screamed Joy.

'No, he's not,' said mother. 'It's all over. Stop being frightened. Look at my arm; there's his sting. Bees only sting once. You're quite safe now.'

Joy stared at the big red weal that was beginning to rise on her mother's arm. She was shaking and very near to tears.

'It's all right, Joy,' said her mother gently. 'It's all over. But next time, do as you're told.'

Miss Fairfax soon extricated the sting, and dabbed the arm with TCP; but Joy was very quiet while she ate her tea, and sat as close to her mother as she could. She kept glancing at the red swelling on her arm, but she did not say anything about it till bedtime, when her mother came to say goodnight.

'I'm sorry, Mummy,' whispered Joy, from somewhere down under the bedclothes. 'I'll never do it again. It was me that ought really to have got stung, wasn't it?'

'Very true,' Mummy replied, 'but all the same, I'm glad it was me.'

'Why?' said Joy, appearing suddenly over the top of the sheet.

'Because I love you,' said Mummy. 'Now, go to sleep.'

Author's Note: *When Jesus stretched out his arms on the cross and said, 'It is finished,' he meant this: 'It's all over. I have paid the price for sin, so that you can be forgiven. By trusting* *in me, you can stop being afraid of death and punishment, because God only punishes sin once. Look at the wounds in my hands - these tell you how much I love you.'*

Keynote: Because of our sins he was wounded, beaten because of the evil we did. We are healed by the punishment he suffered, made whole by the blows he received. Isaiah 53:5

Prayer: Lord Jesus, when I think about all your sufferings and the wounds on your hands, help me to understand how much you loved me. Help me to hate the sin that made you suffer so, for it was I who ought to have suffered. Help me to overcome sin, and turn from it. Teach me to love you, because you loved me so much.

Think: You can show that you love God by loving others. What small things could you do today, to help other people?

Jesus - His death - His righteousness given to us.
2 Corinthians 5:14–21

11. A LIFE FOR A LIFE

This is an old story about two brothers who lived in Spain, many years ago, when law courts were not so careful as they are now.

Luis and Sebastian were twins, and their home was a flat roofed white house outside the walls of a little mountain town. Their parents had died, but had left them a small inheritance, and the boys lived on in their old home. They were so alike that no one in the town could tell them apart.

But as the years passed the boys developed differently. Sebastian held a good job; he was kind, steady and hard-working, and everyone spoke well of him. But Luis was lazy and would not work. He cared for nothing but pleasure, and spent every evening drinking and gambling, often not coming home until early morning. In vain Sebastian begged him to leave his bad companions and make a fresh start. Luis just laughed.

It was late one night, and the full moon shone on the white walls of the town. Sebastian sat at the window, strangely uneasy, his eyes fixed on the white ribbon of road that led to the city gates. Luis, as usual had not come in, but somehow tonight his brother could not sleep.

He spotted the running figure even before he heard the beat of his feet, and he went to the door. Luis was running alone, and pushed past him into the house. By the light of the lamp his face showed deathly white, and his clothes were torn and blood-stained. He trembled so that he could hardly speak.

'Oh Sebastian,' he panted, 'hide me! Hide me! They are coming to take me and it will be death for me!'

'What do you mean?' asked Sebastian, running to the window. Sure enough, a crowd of people were surging from the town gates, running ..... running towards the house.

'We drank too much ...' cried Luis. 'We fought .. I didn't mean to .. he fell back and died. Oh, Sebastian, hide me! What shall I do?'

But Sebastian already knew what to do and was tearing off his tunic. There was not a moment to spare.

'Put on these clothes and give me yours,' he commanded. 'Quick! Stop trembling. Now run out of the back door, and up into the hills, and don't come back for a long time ... run, brother, run!'

Truly, they were only just in time. Already the noise of shouting and running feet was at their gate. A moment later, the town guard, followed by an excited crowd, burst into the house, and drew up short in front of Sebastian. He stood very still, breathing fast, his hair disordered, dirt on his hands and face, wearing the torn, bloodstained tunic. They handcuffed him but he offered no resistance. He walked quietly back to the town jail. A few days later he was tried and condemned to death for murder.

Nearly all the men of the town crowded into that courtroom to gaze at the prisoner. When the trial was over and the spectators sat in the wine houses discussing the case, they all said the same thing:

'How quiet he stood! He did not say a word to defend himself, nor did he plead for his life, nor did he seem afraid.' 'You saw for yourselves the bloodstains on my tunic,' he said. 'I have no defence.'

'And where was that fine brother of his?' asked others. 'Why was he not at the trial? Nor was he at work this morning. Is he ashamed of his brother, that he lets him die alone?'

But no one knew the answer to that one, and a few days later, Sebastian was executed. A life for a life.

Luis hid in the mountain villages for many weeks. He changed his town clothes for a peasant's outfit and worked for a farmer all through the harvest season. At first he never dared leave his lodging; night after night he would wake trembling, dreaming of those terrible running feet. But as time went on he grew bolder. He bitterly regretted killing his comrade and longed to see his brother again. 'Perhaps they will have ceased to hunt for me now,' he thought. 'Next market day I will go down, disguised, to the town and try to speak to my brother.'

He had grown a beard and stained his face, and no one could have recognised him. Dressed in peasant clothing he joined a crowd of muleteers and went to market. While the bargaining was at its height, he joined a group of bystanders, and started chatting. Gradually he drew the conversation round to the recent murder case.

'I hear the wretched fellow got away,' he said. 'Are they still searching for him, or have they given up?'

'Given up?' replied his companion, turning to him in amazement. 'Our militia never give up! They caught him the same day, tried him the same week, and he died two days later. There's justice for you! Strange thing is though, there was a brother who disappeared the same day, and has never turned up since ...some say ..'

But no one ever heard what some were saying, for Luis gave a strange desolate cry and ran from the market place. Half-blinded with tears, he somehow managed to reach the Governor's house and almost forced an entrance. When the Governor appeared to see what the commotion was about, Luis fell at his feet.

'You have killed an innocent man' he cried, over and over again. 'It was I, not my brother. Now take me too, for what have I got to live for now?'

The Governor withdrew. After much discussion, he returned.

'The law says, a life for a life,' he announced. 'If your brother was innocent how could we know - his tunic was covered with blood, and he refused to plead. The case is closed. Go, and keep your mouth shut, and see that you make no more trouble.'

But as Luis turned blindly away, the Governor spoke again. 'Stay,' he said suddenly. 'You are the only brother of the executed man?'

'Yes, yes. There is no one else.'

'Then I have a letter for you. The prisoner wrote it hastily and left it in my care just before he died. I will fetch it for you.'

Seated in the old home where he and his brother had passed so many pleasant evenings together in childhood and early boyhood, Luis wept and wept. It was nearly sunset before he opened the letter. It was very short, and he read it over and over, until it was too dark to see the writing, and he knew it by heart.

'My dear brother,' ran the letter. 'This morning I shall die, of my own free will, in your bloodstained tunic. Now I beseech you to live in my clean tunic. I send you my love and God bless you. Sebastian.'

And Luis understood. The waster, who had lived for himself and fought and murdered, must be counted as dead in prison. The man who had loved and suffered and sacrificed must go on living. It should be so. He sat thinking till the early light glimmered in the room. Then he rose and flung off his dirty disguise. He washed and dressed himself in clean clothing, as Sebastian would have done, and went out to meet the new day.

Author's Note: *Christ, at the cross, took the place of all sinners and died, having clothed himself in our sin. He now tells us to 'clothe' our spirits with the new garments of his love and goodness. When God sees us doing this, he rejoices over us and no longer remembers our sins. For he can then see Jesus living in us as Lord. To all who accept the lordship of Jesus in this way, God opens the gates of heaven.*

Keynote: Christ was without sin, but for our sake God made him share our sin in order that in union with him we might share the righteousness of God. 2 Corinthians 5:21

When anyone is joined to Christ, he is a new being; the old is gone, the new has come. 2 Corinthians 5:17

Prayer: Thank you Lord, that you took my sin so that you could clothe me in your righteousness. Help me day by day to show out the goodness and cleanness and beauty of the Lord Jesus. Teach me to understand how this can be. Teach me to love the one who died for me.

Think: In what practical ways can you show out the goodness and love of Jesus?

I BELIEVE
IN JESUS
CHRIST... WHO
CONQUERED
DEATH WHEN HE
ROSE FROM THE
DEAD

Christ's conquest of death – The Resurrection Story.
Matthew 28:1–10; John 20:1–23

12. THE WAY THROUGH

It was raining torrents for the third day running, and Margaret, glancing out into the dark evening, felt very troubled indeed.

She had motored down from her home on the North African coast, to visit friends in the town of Fez. But that evening she had rung up, and been told that her mother was unwell. She must try and get home next day, but if the rain went on like this the main road would be flooded. When the river rose, the South was sometimes cut off from the North, for as much as a week at a time.

She woke several times in the night only to hear the beating of the rain on the roof, and in the morning the radio confirmed her worst fears. The main roads from North to South were completely flooded. Neither cars, trains nor buses could run.

She studied the map. There was another way, a wild, lonely road that wound up into the mountains; but it also descended into the valleys which might well be flooded too. Her friends advised her to wait, but Margaret was anxious and the weather might well get even worse. She decided to try; after all, she could always come back if it proved impossible.

After travelling for about forty minutes into the wild, high countryside, she began to regret her decision, for she was driving into a thick mist and could see little except for the rocks on her right. She was travelling very slowly when she heard the hooting of a horn, and saw the lights of another car approaching; they drew up side by side on the narrow road and opened their windows.

'What is the road like ahead?' asked Margaret.

'No good,' said the driver in French. 'The river has flooded at the bottom of the hill. I'm going back.'

Two or three other cars followed, but Margaret could not turn on the hilltop. The way ahead sloped down into the mist, so the only thing to do was to drive to the edge of the flood, turn and come back too. Cautiously, hooting her horn, she went down to the plain, and as she approached she heard shouting and the shrill voice of children, and felt glad to be near human life again.

The whole village had turned out to watch the fun, and were standing along the margin of the flood. The river had flowed across the road, a grey swirling waste of water disappearing into the mist. The villagers hailed Margaret with peals of laughter, and three asked for lifts to Fez.

But Margaret badly wanted to go home. She got out and stood on the brink. 'How deep is it?' she asked.

'Nobody knows,' shouted the villagers, delighted that she spoke their language. 'But very, very deep.'

'How far does it go?' asked Margaret again.

'Nobody knows; but, without doubt, very, very far. It is a big river.'

'Has anyone been across it?'

'No, no, nobody. Who would be so foolish? Do we want to drown?'

'Well, I'm going to see,' said Margaret boldly, and in spite of the warnings and consternation of the villagers, she slipped off her shoes and stockings and locked the car. She took a few cautious steps into the flood and the water lapped around her ankles. Oblivious to the frightened commotion behind her, she paddled on, trying each step, her heart beating rather fast. On she went until she was swallowed up in the mist and the villagers reported her drowned; but still the water swirled round her ankles. It seemed a long, cold journey, but when she looked ahead the mists seemed to be clearing a little and there in front of her was the road, climbing up toward the next ridge. And still the water was no deeper than her ankles. A few minutes later she stepped ashore. She went back rather quicker that she had come, and could hear the excitement on the shore before she could see anything.

'Ah foolish woman!' they cried. 'The flood has swept her away. Did we not tell her?'

Then suddenly a great yell went up, and their consternation changed to merriment as the dripping, bedraggled figure waded in through the mist .. A lorry and two cars had arrived by this time, and were waiting to see what would happen. They hailed Margaret joyfully.

'Is it really possible to go through?' they shouted.

'Perfectly possible,' replied Margaret. 'It is not above my ankles anywhere. The mists are breaking on the other side, and the road runs high for a long way.'

'Yes, yes,' called the lorry driver, who knew the roads well. 'If we can cross this we shall reach the highway beyond the floods. Come, Mademoiselle, when you are ready we will all cross over together.'

So, to the cheering of the crowd, the cavalcade passed over with the water splashing round their wheels and came out, laughing, on to the rising road. And as they climbed the mists parted, and pale sun broke through. At the top of the hill, Margaret turned and looked back and gasped. For the grey flood she had feared so much, sparkled like a sheet of silver, and over the washed, shining mountains hung a rainbow.

Author's Note: *A famous man called Roger Bacon once said, 'Men fear death as children fear to go out into the dark.' No human being has ever been through death and come back to tell others what happens - except one! Jesus. He entered into death, and his disciples thought they would never see him again. But they were wrong. Three days later he returned, alive and risen, and showed himself to many of his followers. He was the only one to go right through* *death and come back and tell us that those who love and follow him need never fear it. Through Jesus, death leads to eternal life with God.*

Keynote: Jesus said, 'I am the resurrection and the life. Whoever believes in me will live, even though he dies; whoever lives and believes in me will never die. Do you believe this?' John 11:25,26

I am the living one. I was dead, but now I am alive for ever and ever. I have authority over death and the world of the dead.' Revelation 1:18

Prayer: Lord, I am thankful that you went right through death and came back to tell us not to be afraid. I am glad that for those who love and trust you death is just the last part of the way home. Thank you for the joy of those who have gone ahead. Thank you that we shall see them again.

Think: Do you believe that the resurrection of Jesus really happened? If you do, how does it affect your life? What does death mean to you? - What difference does Jesus make to you as you think about death?

13. THE VOICE IN THE DARK

'Are you sure you don't mind coming home alone, Rachel?' asked Mother. 'I'll tell Bill to come and meet you if you like.'

Rachel shook her head hard. Her father always picked her up on his way home from work, but that afternoon he and her mother were going out. Rachel had been worrying about this for days, because it would be nearly dark when she came out of school, and she hated the thought of that little back lane just before she got home. The trees met overhead and made strange, frightening noises on windy evenings. If she was late, it might be quite dark.

Only one thing would be worse than having to run down that lane alone, and that was to have Bill, her younger brother, come and fetch her. Bill was extremely tough and feared nothing so he was always teasing Rachel because she was afraid of spiders and cows and other things. If Bill discovered she was also afraid of the back lane she would never hear the end of it.

All day long the thought of the twilit lane bothered Rachel, and kept her mind from her lessons. Worst of all the day which had begun so brightly was clouding over, and the wind was rising. At half past three they turned on the lights in the classroom, and outside there was a growl of thunder.

'Will anyone going in for a music exam, please stay behind for a few minutes after school?' Rachel's heart sank at the announcement. That would mean quite a long delay, for her name came near the end of the list. And it was almost dark now. The other children were hurrying to get home before the storm.

By the time Rachel left the building it was dark and raining and the street lamps were lighted. There were plenty of people about and nothing to be afraid of yet. Only the wind swept round the street corners blowing the drops in her face, and she wondered what it would sound like whistling through the branches that met over the lane.

And now she had reached the place where she must turn off the road and into the tunnel of trees. A clap of thunder startled her and terror overtook her. Even Bill's jokes would have been welcome now. She was sure that evil things, and perhaps bad men, lurked in those shadows waiting to pounce. She stood rigid, trying to fight down her fears and make a run for it. It was such a short way.

And then, above the howling of the wind and the drive of the rain, she heard a voice calling her name: 'Are you there Rachel?' And she knew the voice. With a little sob of relief she plunged into the shadows and hurled herself into her father's arms.

'Steady little girl!' said her father, rather surprised. 'Anything the matter?'

'No,' whispered Rachel, still trembling. 'I just thought ... well, I just thought you weren't there!'

'Well, I wasn't,' said Daddy, 'but we came home early, and found you weren't in. I didn't like the idea of you being out all alone in the storm, so I came. Come on, let's get home quick!'

So they hurried along the lane together, and Rachel hardly noticed the howling of the wind because she was telling her father how she had scored a goal at netball. And she quite forgot the fierce creatures waiting to pounce from behind the trees, because she was holding tight to her father's hand.

Author's Note: *The three days following Jesus's death must have been terrible for the disciples. After having known him for three years, they suddenly found themselves alone, in danger of maybe also being killed, but in any case, whether* *life or death, they were convinced that it would have to be faced without the master. For this Jesus whom they had trusted, had failed in his mission and had finally suffered a dreadful death. So it was to very frightened men that, on the evening of the third day, Jesus suddenly appeared. Standing in the middle of the group, alive and strong, he stretched out his hands, saying, 'Peace be with you. Look at my hands and feet, and see that it is I myself.' As they looked at the pierced hands of Jesus, the disciples began to realise that his power was greater even than the power of death.*

Keynote: The disciples were filled with joy at seeing the Lord. John 20:20

Prayer: Lord Jesus, I am so glad that you came back from the dead and that you are alive today. I thank you that, if you are with me, I need never feel lonely or afraid, and that nothing can really hurt me if I walk through my life with you. Keep me very close to you all my life, until you take me to your Home.

Think: Do you sometimes feel afraid? Think about that frightening situation and then imagine the Lord right in it, holding out his hand and saying, 'Peace ... it is I myself.'

WHERE DO YOU STAND?

So far, we have tried to understand more about God as Father and Creator. We then looked at the way he came to us in Jesus, focusing on how Jesus lived to leave an example for us, died to save us, and rose again to be our living Friend and remain with us through life, death and eternity.

God has done all this for every single person, and this includes you. Maybe you still find these facts too new and difficult to grasp for the time being, and feel the need for more thought, opportunity to talk with others, and prayer. But if at this stage you believe what has been covered so far, and genuinely want to become God's child, you will want to know how you can become a Christian. There are three main steps you must take:

To commit myself to Jesus Christ I need to

- repent of my sin
- believe in, and wholly give myself to him
- receive his Holy Spirit into my heart.

Repentance, the theme of the next three narratives means that:

- I recognise my sin
- I confess my sin to God
- I turn away from my sin.

14. WHITER THAN SNOW

Aisha lived in a North African village. Her husband had many goats and a few cows and she was better off than most of her neighbours. They mostly lived in thatched huts and fetched their water from the village well and washed their clothes in the stream in the valley. But Aisha's house had a flat concrete roof and a stove attached to cylinder gas; she washed the family's clothes under her own fig tree and hung them to dry on her own roof.

She was proud and happy for nearly everything she possessed was a little better than what anyone else had. Other people went to market on mules or jogged three or four miles on foot and caught the local bus, but her husband had an old car, and she drove to town in style.

It was on a cold dull December day that they came home from market. For the last half mile the road degenerated into a rough track but she hardly noticed the jolting for she was looking over her purchases. Most of the village women washed with great yellow bars of soap, but she had seen an advertisement for a soap powder, which claimed to 'wash whiter'. She loved her children's clothes to look cleaner than anyone else's, and she had a big wash waiting. She hoped the weather would hold, for a bitter north wind whistled through the gorges of the hills behind the village.

Aisha was glad to get home, call in her children and put on the kettle. She woke early next morning and heated the water. She worked hard and soon the clothing was hanging out on the roof for the whole village to see. Aisha looked round contentedly. Across the track her neighbour had spread out some ragged little garments on the prickly pear hedge, but they looked poor and dingy compared with hers.

Her powder really did wash whiter.

It got colder and colder; the sky over the mountain was a strange light grey, the peaks looked near and menacing. Nothing was dry by nightfall and families huddled round the glowing charcoal and went to bed early. When they woke the sun was shining and Aisha gave her children their breakfast and sent them off to school. Then she climbed the outside staircase to look at her washing. Surely it would shine dazzling white in the sun - so white that all the village would turn and gaze at its purity and wonder. She opened the door of the roof and stood transfixed. 'Who's been soiling my washing?' she cried angrily, striding forward.

Then she stopped and understood. No one had soiled her washing; but snow had fallen in the night and the mountains behind her home were covered in dazzling white, too bright to look at. Against that sparkling purity her sheets looked almost grey. 'Truly, they are nothing to God's whiteness,' she muttered, pulling them down in a hurry. But as she turned her back on those shining summits, she caught sight of the rags on the prickly pear bush and felt comforted.

Author's Note: *If you compare yourself with others you always find someone who is less well brought up, less fortunate and less well-behaved than you. That makes you feel good. But when we look at the shining, pure loving life of Jesus we can't feel good any longer. We realise how far we fall short of his standards. To really look at Jesus and to think about his life, teaches me that I am a sinner.*

Keynote: How stupid they are! They make up their own standards to measure themselves by, and they judge themselves by their own standards. 2 Corinthians 10:12

Prayer: Lord as I read the Gospels and look at the love, truth and goodness of the Lord Jesus, help me to see how far I've fallen short of what you meant me to be. Let me stop comparing myself with other people and compare myself with you instead. Make me sorry for my life which is so unlike Jesus, and help me to become a better person.

Think: When I read about the perfect life of Jesus, what does it show me about myself?

15. THE BARRIER

Zohra lived in a shack near the seashore on the Atlantic coast of North Africa. Her husband was an invalid and she had no children. But she did odd jobs here and there, begged a little, collected driftwood on the beach and somehow managed.

Then a strange thing happened in that little seaside town. A European doctor started a dispensary in the white house out near the sand dunes, and many people went to him to be treated. Zohra herself decided to go along and ask for a bottle of medicine for her husband because he was too feeble to go himself.

It was a pleasant place, this new dispensary, clean and quiet. People sat on benches and waited and there was no pushing aside of the poor, no shouting and nobody asking for bribes. Zohra sat patiently by the open window looking out into an enclosed garden vivid with geraniums and nasturtiums, and as she watched, a tiny fair-haired girl toddled out to play under the fig tree. A moment later her sister, a little older, but just like her, followed her.

As she watched them , Zohra suddenly had a wonderful idea. These two little girls were playing with the earth; their clothes would get dirty and their father wore a white coat. Surely they would need a washer woman, and surely this dispensary would need scrubbing every day! She forgot about the bottle of medicine and slipped round the door of the house and knocked. A fair-haired young woman came to the door and asked her, in very faltering Arabic, what she wanted.

'I have come to be your washer-woman,' said Zohra. ' I will wash your clothes as white as milk; I will scrub and cook. I will come every day.'

The young woman laughed. 'As a matter of fact,' she said, 'I do need a washer-woman. Come back tomorrow when I have talked to my husband.'

Zohra went home walking on air. She was sure she would get that job; she and that young woman had somehow clicked, and those funny little girls with heads like yellow chickens had smiled up at her too. But as she neared the house she saw something even better than the prospect of a job. Someone had left the gate open at the big house next to hers; a fat hen had strayed into the road and was scratching the dust in a leisurely sort of way.

It was certainly Zohra's lucky day. She looked all around but there was no one in sight. The hen was tame and friendly and clucked at her feet. She snatched it up, hid it under the folds of her voluminous white haik, and hurried into her own little home. She showed her prize to her husband who was delighted. It was a long time since he had had a good meat meal, and he lumbered out into the yard and cut the hen's throat; Zohra plucked it in no time and buried its feathers in the sand. Then she blew up the charcoal, and it was soon bubbling in the pot along with parsley, onions, carrots and spices. Oh, it had been a wonderful day!

After making a few enquiries, the young English woman took Zohra on trial, and Zohra was happier than she had ever been before. She loved the sweet milky coffee that she drank each morning on arrival, and she loved the two tiny girls with hair like chicken-down. But one thing she could not understand. Every day as she finished her coffee, her mistress would sit down beside her and read her something about Jesus Christ from her own Holy book.

'Does she think I can read or understand at my age?' chuckled Zohra. 'Can an old cat learn to dance?' and at first she neither listened nor remembered. She switched off. But the Word of God is alive and powerful and has a way of piercing through indifference.

After a few weeks she found herself remembering things

she had not even known she was listening to: that story, for instance, about 5,000 people supping off five loaves and two fishes! That was a splendid story, and she told it to her husband; and that one about a sheep that got lost. Very gradually she found herself looking forward to these stories, hungry and restless if she had to miss them, and she hardly realised that she was beginning to love the one who had healed the blind and raised the dead, and even more slowly was she coming to understand that he was still alive, there, invisible beside them as they read about him; there, in the house where he was loved and welcomed, and because of him there was peace and gentleness and laughter in the home, and she loved to be there and hated to leave.

She wanted him too, and her mistress never got tired of telling her that he wanted her. It almost dazed her to think about it, but one summer evening when she was alone in the house, she went out and sat on the step and looked out over the quiet sea. Jesus seemed near, and she knew now what she had to do - ask him into her heart and commit herself fully to his way. Perhaps she would do it right there ... but even as she made the decision she seemed to see a white hen clucking in the dust, and to smell the chicken stew.

'If we confess our sin he is faithful and just to forgive us our sins and to cleanse us from all unrighteousness.' Her mistress had taught her that. Her joy faded, for somehow she knew that that little white hen stood as a barrier between her and her Lord, and she could not get past it. Everything was spoiled. She went indoors and quarrelled with her husband and could not sleep.

And then the most amazing thought came to her: she could do something about the barrier. She had never heard of anyone doing such a thing before but she supposed it could be done. On Friday her mistress paid her, and on Friday she would get rid of that wretched little white hen.

On Friday she got home early, dressed herself in her best clothes and slipped through into the little poultry farm . She knew the man would be at work, but it was the woman, her neighbour, she wanted to see. Sitting beside her on a low mattress, hands clasped, tears streaming down her cheek, Zohra told her story.

'Oh, my sister, forgive me!' she pleaded. 'I will buy you a turkey or a duck, or anything you want .. only forgive me.'

The woman was staring at her in amazement. The hen and even the money was temporarily forgotten in the sheer craziness of what was happening. 'But I'd never have known,' she gasped. 'Why, why, oh why did you come and tell me?'

'One day,' whispered the woman, 'I will tell you; but not now.'

She slipped the price of the hen into her neighbour's hand and hurried home. She had an appointment to keep and there was no barrier now.

Keynote: If we confess our sins to God, he will keep his promise and do what is right: he will forgive us our sins and purify us from all our wrongdoing. (1 John 1:9)

Prayer: Lord, I know that you cannot cleanse what I hide, so I want to tell you about the wrong things in my life. Thank you that as I confess them you have promised to forgive. Thank you too for forgiving those sins I have forgotten about. If I have wronged another person, help me to put it right with them as well as with you. If I have taken what is not mine, help me to give it back. If I have told a lie help me to say that it was not true. If I have quarrelled or hurt anyone, help me to say I am sorry.

Think: Make a point of carrying out what you have just prayed for, trusting God to give you courage. Can you see a difference between remorse and repentance?

16. THE FIVE FINGER PRAYER

Andrew had been travelling for hours through the backwoods of northern Canada, and he was tired when he reached the little log hotel where the trappers and the company officials put up on their journeys. He loved these drives, mile after mile through the green gloom of great trees. He was on his way to preach at a settlement further north and he welcomed the thought of a quiet evening.

But it was not to be. No sooner had he signed in, than the hotel manager came towards him with outstretched hands. 'Pastor Jackson,' he said, his face beaming; 'They told me up at the settlement that you'd be coming through today. It's real good to have you; come in for a hot drink.'

Andrew Jackson could not refuse such a warm invitation, and sitting beside the proprietor, he heard this story. Here was a lonely Christian couple too isolated to attend any church regularly, delighted at the coming of the Pastor. The family begged him to have supper with them and over the table the host suggested that, as he was not in a hurry to leave early, he should invite the few guests in the hotel to stay for family prayers after breakfast.

'I should be glad to lead them,' said Andrew, 'but I should like your staff to come too. As I went up to my room earlier I passed a woman with such a sad face cleaning a window. When I greeted her she turned away, but I can't forget the sorrow in her eyes.'

'Oh her!' said the proprietor thoughtfully. 'She is of Indian origin, and has had great tragedies in her life. I really keep her out of pity, for she has lost the will to work. I don't think I could bring her in with my guests; she never bothers to clean or tidy.'

'Let her sit just by the door if she will,' urged Andrew. 'I should like her to be there.'

Next morning the guests were surprised when a short service was announced after breakfast, but most stayed for they too, in their lonely travels, were seldom near a church. They listened politely, and a few thanked the Pastor warmly but only one stayed to question him, and that was the sad-faced woman who sat unnoticed in the doorway. When the other guests had left the dining room she followed the Pastor into the passage. 'Sir,' she whispered, 'I never hear it put like that before. Could you teach me a little prayer? I'm not educated, you know, but I should like to pray.'

'Yes,' said Andrew gently, 'I will teach you a prayer. You must say it every day till I return in a week's time, and then I will see you again.'

'A very short prayer, Sir. I'm no scholar and I can't remember much. It must be very short.'

'It is very short; it is just five words, one for each finger of your hand so that you cannot forget it. Say them after me ... one word for each finger ... O Lord, show me myself.'

The Pastor drove off into the deep forest, but a week later he was back. When he had greeted his host he enquired for the window-cleaner.

The proprietor sighed. 'She seems a lot worse than she was before; every time I see her she is crying into her bucket. I shall have to get rid of her if she goes on like this. It upsets the others.'

The Pastor went to search for her and found her carrying out her duties. 'Well,' he said, 'I've come back. Did you remember the prayer, and did you say it?'

The tears sprang to her eyes and she clasped her hands.

'Every day I have said it,' she whispered, 'and every day it gets worse; every day I remember more wrong I have done, and every day my heart gets heavier, oh, what shall I do?'

'I will tell you what to do. Do not pray that prayer any more at present. I am going to teach you another one.'

'Just a short one, Sir. Don't forget I am no scholar. I can't remember much.'

'A very short one; just five words again, like the last one; one word for each finger of your hand ...say it after me .. O Lord, show me yourself.'

'And for how long shall I say this prayer Sir?'

'You can say it every day, for the rest of your life.'

Some years later the pastor, Andrew Jackson, visited the district again to preach in a new church near the settlement. Almost everyone attended, and the visitor was particularly struck by the bright faces of the young people, and the way they sang. When he commented on it the new Pastor said, 'Yes, I'm very thankful for our young people, but I've only helped. They have mostly been brought in by a couple who live in the district. They married not long ago and they do wonderful work among the children and teenagers. She is like a second mother to them all. It's a strange story. She is of Indian origin and has very little education...'

'I should like to meet her,' said Andrew.

A dark-haired woman dressed in attractive clothes stepped forward smiling, and clasped his hand. 'Do you remember me, Sir?', she asked. Then, seeing the doubt in his face, she laughed. 'I did not expect you to recognise me,' she said, 'but you will remember the prayer, one word for each finger.'

Recognition dawned in his eyes, but she went on speaking eagerly.

'I've prayed that prayer every day since you left me .. he's shown me himself .. I am learning to love him more and more .. oh Sir, I shall go on praying that prayer every day till I see him.'

This woman not only saw her sin and confessed her sin, but she turned from her sin to Jesus. Because she knew that all her wrongdoing of the past was forgiven, she left the old, sad ways behind her and started on a new life, filled with the joy of being free to look not behind, but ahead.

Keynote: Here are two prayers that David prayed in the Psalms-

Remove my sin, and I will be clean; wash me, and I will be whiter than snow .. Close your eyes to my sins and wipe out all my evil. Create a clean heart in me, and put a new and loyal spirit in me. Psalm 51:7-10

Examine me, O God, and know my mind; test me, and discover my thoughts. Find out if there is any evil in me and guide me in the everlasting way.
Psalm 139:23,24

Think: What two important lessons can we learn from this story?

17. THE CAPTAIN AND THE CABIN BOY

Captain Brown lived in the days of sailing ships, and his beautiful vessel was one of the finest in the Merchant Navy. He had sailed all round the world, trading, and his daring and iron discipline were proverbial. His crew were a foul-mouthed, hard-drinking lot who feared nothing. You needed to be tough to sail with Captain Brown or you did not last long.

He was as dauntless as ever, yet there were those who whispered that the captain was past it and should be put ashore. But they whispered it very softly, for had he heard them he would have pitched them overboard. No one was going to tell Captain Brown when to retire. His vessel, the Golden Eagle, set out on a calm Atlantic Ocean one summer's day. 'It should not take long to cross with a favourable wind and then I'll consult one of those American doctors, maybe,' said Captain Brown to himself, 'for I'm not feeling as good as I ought to; but shore's an unhealthy place, and maybe the sea breezes will put me to rights.' But they didn't, and after a few days he found he could no longer bark out his angry orders - too short of breath; and climbing up into the crow's nest made him so giddy that he decided not to risk it again. He retired into his cabin, growling like an angry old lion, and sent for the First Mate.

'You'll have to take over for a day or two,' mumbled the Captain irritably. 'Just a touch of bronchitis! The sea breezes will put me on my feet in no time.' But he slept little that night and in the morning the ship's doctor came to see him. He told him to rest for a few days and no doubt the sea air would put him right. But outside the cabin the doctor shook his head at the First Mate. 'I don't think the old man will reach shore,' he said. 'His chest is terribly congested, and pneumonia is setting in. Still, he'd lie easier in the ocean than under the earth - never was much of a land-lubber.'

Inside the cabin Captain Brown also knew quite well that the sea breezes would never revive him. In a way he was not sorry for he had always wanted to die at sea; but he'd been a hard-drinking, foul-mouthed old man and now it was all over. For the first time in many years he began to wonder what would happen next. If there was a God he was in no state to meet him, and he began to worry. Had he been ashore he could have gone to church or sent for a parson or borrowed a Bible. But here on his own ship, if he'd found any of his crew reading a Bible, he'd have tossed it into the sea. So he dozed all day, haunted by strange dreams, and when he awoke in the evening he knew that he was worse, and his worry increased. When the First Mate came in for orders, he asked abruptly, 'Has anyone on this ship got a Bible?'

The First Mate stared. 'The old man's delirious!' he thought to himself.

The captain drew himself a little further up on the pillow. 'I said,' he gasped angrily, 'has anyone on this ship got a Bible? Can you give me a straight answer to a straight question?'

'N...n...no, sir, I don't suppose so,' faltered the First Mate. 'I could go and ask, sir if you like.'

'Go!' muttered the Captain,'and don't come back without one.'

When the crew heard that the Captain wanted a Bible they thought it was a great joke. But the First Mate was in no laughing mood. He feared for his own reception.

'What does he think we are?' shouted one, 'a Sunday School?' But this started a new train of thought. He considered for a moment.

'Just a minute,' he said. 'Talking about Sunday School ... there's a new little cabin boy, Joe Prescott. I've seen him down among the hammocks reading something. Delicate little chap he looks, but he works well...'

'Fetch him,' barked the First Mate, and a moment later Jo Prescott, cabin boy, and the youngest member of the ship's crew, stood quaking in front of the Officer.

'Joe Prescott?'

'Y ..... yes, Sir'

'I hear you have been seen reading down among the hammocks.'

'Only when my work's done, Sir'

'What do you read?'

'My Bible, Sir'

'I see; well, fetch your Bible and take it straight to the Captain's cabin. Say I sent you, and hurry.'

The child's face turned rather white. He was terrified of the captain, but there was nothing to do but to obey at a run. And there was another fear, even worse than his fear of the captain. Supposing they took his Bible away from him?

He hurried across the deck, clasping his precious book, and knocked at the cabin door. But it was not the usual gruff bark that bade him enter. It was a weary, breathless voice, and when Joe got inside he hardly recognised his Captain. The spent figure lying on the bed was quite unlike the angry, blustering Captain Brown. Joe's fear gave place to a great pity as he stood at attention waiting for the Captain to speak.

'Who are you?'

'Joe Prescott, Sir; cabin boy.'

'Who told you to come?'

'First Mate, Sir. He told me to bring my Bible.'

'Ah yes, a Bible!' the tired voice was eager. 'Sit down, boy, sit down! I can't read myself .. my sights gone dim .. read me something out of that Bible.. I may never reach port.'

Joe thumbed nervously through his Bible, for he could see that the old man was very ill. He came at last to John, chapter three, and the story of Nicodemus, who longed to see the Kingdom of God. He read slowly and distinctly, but the Captain's eyes were closed and he showed no sign of understanding. So when Joe came to verse sixteen he read it very slowly indeed. 'For God loved the world so much that he gave his only Son, so that everyone who believes in him may not die but have eternal life.'

The Captain opened his eyes and stared. Jo was emboldened to speak; 'Please Sir' he said, 'may I read that verse in the way my mother told me to read it?'

'Read it anyhow you like, boy,' said the Captain, 'only get on! The time may be short.' So Joe read the verse again.

'For God loved Joe Prescott so much that he gave his only Son, so that if Jo believes in him, Jo may not die but have eternal life.'

The Captain had turned toward him. His eyes were fixed on the child, and he was breathing fast.

'Read it again, boy,' he whispered, 'read it again .. and put your Captain's name in it.'

So Joe read it again; 'For God loved Captain Brown so much that he gave his only Son, so that if Captain Brown believes in him, Captain Brown may not die but have eternal life.'

'That's it,' muttered the Captain. 'That's the anchor! That'll get me into port!'

So Joe Prescott slipped away, his precious Bible hidden under his uniform, and the old Captain turned his face toward the Heavenly Harbour.

Author's Note: *We have seen how God came down to us in Jesus, and died to make payment for the sins of the world, and rose again to be our Saviour and Friend. However, none of this will be of any help to you unless you, too, come to him with your sin and believe in him as your Saviour and Friend.*

Keynote: For God loved ... so much that he gave his only Son, so that if ... believes in him, ... may not die but have eternal life. John 3:16

Prayer: Lord, I know that you loved the world and died to save sinners from their sin. So today I bring my sin to your cross. I want to confess it and turn away from it. I want to be forgiven. I believe that you love me. I take you now as my own Saviour, and I give myself to you to be yours for ever. I put my name into the verse.

Think: Do you feel that you can say with both your heart and your mind, 'The Son of God loved me and gave his life for me' ? Galatians 2:20

I BELIEVE IN THE HOLY SPIRIT - GOD'S PRESENCE IN US

18. THE KNOCK ON THE DOOR

Maggie had lived all her married life within sight of the great castle on the hill. Her husband had brought her to the cottage on the riverbank as a bride, and there she had borne and reared her family. Soon after her arrival, Prince Albert had rebuilt the castle of true Scottish granite. The massive tower, surmounted by its turret, dominated the landscape, looking at a distance as though hewn out of one solid rock. Behind it rose the peak of Craig-gowan, and in front the Royal acres sloped gently down to the banks of the Dee. The neighbours considered Maggie a fortunate woman, for her husband was chosen to work as a gardener on the estate, and he brought home good wages regularly.

'She's a guid mistress for all she's a Queen,' Robbie would often say when he came home at night, and Maggie and the bairns would gather round and ask questions. And when the Royal family were in residence, what tales he had to tell!

They nearly always came up in the summer when the hills were purple with heather and the rowans beginning to turn. Then in the evenings Robbie and Maggie and the children would sit on the bench and on the stools on the porch - the honeysuckle porch looked west toward the sunset, and the father would smoke his pipe and recount every detail of the day: the wee princesses had been skipping in the garden - no, daddy was never very good at remembering what their dresses looked like - and those bonny princes in their kilts had ridden out with their father, the Prince Consort. Her Majesty, still a young woman in those early days, often walked in her gardens and she always greeted Robbie and enquired after his wife and bairns. Sometimes they had parties and Robbie would tell of carriages and plumes and beautiful ladies, and sometimes he would be told to carry flowers to the castle, and then he would catch a glimpse of what the cooks were doing. Little Andy, who was fat and greedy, liked hearing about that best of all. How they would laugh at him, sitting on his father's knee, sniffing and licking his lips over imaginary banquets.

But those happy years passed. Prince Albert died and the Queen seemed to grow old overnight, and there were no more lively parties and balls at Balmoral. But Robbie still worked in the gardens as faithfully as ever, until one winter he came home coughing. He died of pneumonia just before Christmas and they buried him under the snow, and her Majesty grieved for her gardener and sent a letter of appreciation. She also arranged a pension for his wife, and this was a great comfort, for they were both widows now.

The children grew up and left home one by one to marry in other glens or to work in the cities. They begged their mother to go and live with them, but she could not tear herself away from the cottage and the castle and Robbie's grave. So they often visited her instead, except in winter when the roads were blocked with snow, and then Maggie stayed alone with her thoughts and her rheumatism.

Then there came a terrible winter. No one in the village remembered such cold weather. They had been snowbound for days on end and food and fuel were scarce and expensive. Maggie had her pension, but somehow it had melted away in the cold season. The roof had leaked and she had had to get it mended, and she'd paid a laddie twice to shovel snow from her path. Now, for the first time ever, she was in debt, and she dared not go on buying food at the village store when she could no longer pay for what she had already bought. The oatmeal barrel was nearly empty and so was the flour bin. Her fire burned low but she dare not put on more coal. Her heart was as grey and desolate as the low skies over the snow.

'Oh Robbie, Robbie,' she cried, 'if you hadna' left me it wouldna' been like this.'

A knock at the door made her start. Whoever would call on a day like this? An awful suspicion crossed her mind - maybe it was the grocer himself come up to ask for payment of her bill. Shame swept over her. She could not face the respectable Mr MacPherson and tell him that she could not pay for ten days at least. She would slip into the back kitchen and close the door, and after a while he would go away and in this weather he would not be likely to call again in a hurry.

Another knock, rather peremptory. She was glad she had drawn the curtains. She rose and tiptoed into the kitchen, laughing a little. She'd not go to her own front door unless she pleased. No one could force her.

But standing behind her kitchen door her heart smote her. Just supposing it was someone in trouble! There was Mrs MacPhail up the hill whose wee Jeanie was so ill ... supposing she was knocking on the door to say Jeanie had died? Or suppose it was some poor body in the snow needing shelter?

Another knock, much louder! She ran across the parlour, flung open the door and nearly fell backwards in surprise. There was a fine carriage in the street and all the neighbours were at their doors wrapped in shawls and curtseying. And on her doorstep stood a footman in Royal livery carrying a great basket, while her Majesty herself, small and regal, smiled and nodded from the window of the carriage.

Just a few words of sympathy, and a sentence of appreciation for Robbie's years of service, and the horses plodded on to another cottage. But the great basket had been lifted over the threshold and in it was all she would need for a long time to come. But it was not the warm shawl or the packet of tea nor the oatmeal nor the substantial gift of money that brought tears running down Maggie's furrowed cheeks. It was something else.

'She came herself!' murmured Maggie over and over again. 'Her Majesty came herself and I never kenned. Thank the Lord, oh thank the good Lord, I opened the door.'

Author's Note: *The Queen stopped for a few minutes at Maggie's door, but God's Holy Spirit, whom Jesus promised to his disciples before he left this earth, wants to come into our hearts and stay there forever. The Holy Spirit loves to dwell in a clean, forgiven heart. Through his new life, we are born again. Through his new life we can grow as Christians.*

Keynote: I will ask the Father, and he will give you another helper, who will stay with you forever. John 14:16
Listen! I stand at the door and knock; if anyone hears my voice and opens the door, I will come into his house. Revelation 3:20

Prayer: Oh come to my heart, Lord Jesus, there is room in my heart for you.

Think: Are you aware of the Holy Spirit working in your life? In what particular ways are you learning to recognise his voice?

19. THE FRIEND WHO REMEMBERED

Bruce and Peter were great friends. They sat side by side at school and did their homework together, too, as Bruce was brighter than Peter and liked to help him. In holiday time they went trainspotting together, and shared a small allotment and sold vegetables to their friends. They were only children, and their mothers grew used to having two boys instead of one, though they mostly went to Bruce's house, because Peter's home was not a happy one, and his mother was so taken up with her own troubles she hardly seemed to notice her son.

The years passed. Bruce came top of his class, but Peter had to repeat the year. It wasn't so easy to be together and, although Bruce wanted to help, Peter did not seem to want to bother. Besides, Bruce had to work hard for his own exams ... gradually they drifted apart.

Bruce went to college and took up law. Peter tried job after job, but he seemed unable to make a success of anything, and his father nagged him so that he no longer went home. He took a room down town next to his favourite public house, and lived as best as he could. He married at one point, but his wife soon tired of his ways and left him. So more years passed, and when Bruce was appointed a local magistrate and bought a large house for himself and his family on the hill behind the town, Peter decided not to go and call.

But they were soon destined to meet, for the law had its eye on Peter. On one or two occasions he had been taken to the Police Station for being drunk and disorderly, and there had been other little incidents too. He had a small job, but found it hard to live and have enough over for his drink and cigarettes, so he had taken to shop-lifting; just a little at a time from the food counters. He was very careful and had never been caught until the day when the police accosted him outside Marks and Spencers and asked to look in his bag. He was sorry they'd got those sausages off him; he'd been looking forward to frying them for supper.

He'd been to court before, and it didn't worry him too much, for somehow he felt so tired these days that nothing seemed worth worrying about except not having enough to drink. No one else cared so why should he? Only one thing really bothered him, and that was the thought of meeting Bruce. 'But maybe it'll be someone else,' he said to himself. 'And even if it is him, he's probably forgotten me.'

But it wasn't someone else. There he was all togged up in his best suit and there was no telling whether Bruce had forgotten or not, for Peter made a point of not meeting those steady grey eyes he remembered so well. 'Only person who ever really bothered about me,' he thought to himself rather vaguely, and the voice pronouncing his fine seemed strangely far away. It was a larger fine than he expected too, and he'd never get it together. Oh well! Prison would be a change!

He felt rather bitter as he let himself into his dingy room later that evening. He'd sometimes dreamed of sprucing himself up a bit and going to call on Bruce, but this was the end to that little flight of fancy. He suddenly hated his old friend. He could have got him off if he'd wanted to - extenuating circumstances, and all the rest of it; but Bruce had done the worst. He went to the cupboard and deliberately tore up the little packet of letters that had lain there for a long while. He and Bruce had written to each other for several years after leaving school.

He flung himself down on the bed and gave way to bitter thoughts. He did not switch on the light and it was quite dark when he heard the knock. 'If it's the old girl for the rent, it's not due for another three days,' he muttered and took no notice. But whoever it was went on knocking, rather a timid knock, not at all like the impatient rat-tat-tat of his landlady. He got up, switched on the light and opened the door. There was a long silence. 'Can I come in, Pete?' said Bruce at last.

'Please yourself,' said Peter. He was staring at his friend. Bruce, without his collar and tie, looked different, just an ordinary man in a polo-necked pullover; broader and greying a little, but not unlike the bright-faced boy who had helped him with his maths.

'Make yourself at home,' said Peter.

'Thanks,' said Bruce. There was another silence, broken at last by Bruce.

'Pete,' he said, 'do you remember the allotment?'

'You bet. Have a drink?'

'Thanks.' Another silence, while Peter uncorked a bottle. It was easier to talk while they sipped their drinks.

'Pete, have you a job?'

'Job? No; jail's my next job; how d'you imagine I'll pay that fine?'

'Well, that's what I came about. The fine's paid Peter ... and I can't cope with the garden. It's much too big, and it's gone to ruin. You were always a better gardener than me, Pete. D'you remember how the slugs made for my lettuces, and I could never think why? I just wondered ... There's a little bungalow adjoining the house, and you could do market gardening in quite a big way. It would be fun to be together again. Would you consider it?'

'How do you know I wouldn't steal your wife's diamond tiara?' retorted Pete, but he chuckled. He had always loved gardening.

'When will you come?' asked Bruce. 'Tomorrow?'

'I'll think about it,' said Peter. 'Thanks a lot.'

He stood at the window and watched Bruce drive off into the rain, but his thoughts were already busy. He knew the garden; he'd often looked over the hedge and imagined what he could make of it. There was a sunny wall ideal for fruit trees, and a sheltered bed where he could put in strawberry plants. He stood for a very long time at that window just staring; but he wasn't seeing the blurred street lamps, nor the rain bouncing on the pavement. He was standing in early autumn sunshine, surrounded by the bitter-sweet smell of chrysanthemums. He was watching the butterflies on the michaelmas daisies.

Author's Note: *The judge who condemned and the man who paid the debt and the friend who gave Peter a new start in life were all the same person. In the same way, God will one day judge and punish sin, and because he is a righteous judge, not one sin will be forgotten. The wages of sin is 'eternal death', which means being separated from God, and these wages must be paid. But God, the Judge, laid aside his robes of glory and came to us in Jesus; he paid the debt of sin once and for all when he died on the Cross. He now comes to us by the Holy Spirit and asks us to receive him into our hearts, and start a new life with him, forgiven and joyful.*

Keynote: He died for all, so that those who live should no longer live for themselves but only for him who died and was raised to life for their sake... (Therefore) when anyone is joined to Christ, he is a new being; the old is gone, the new has come. 2 Corinthians 5:15,17

Prayer: Thank you, Lord, that you paid my debt at Calvary. Thank you that you came back from the dead to offer me a new start. You have given me your Holy Spirit so that my life may be useful, worthwhile and purposeful. Help me to turn away from the things that spoil my life. Teach me to live close to you and work for you. Thank you for this wonderful second start.

Think: Have you personally experienced this new beginning in your life? If you have, in what ways are you trusting the Holy Spirit to help you make a fresh start?

THE WORK OF THE HOLY SPIRIT - GOD'S POWER IN US

20. THE MESSENGER

It was a beautiful spot where Harry and Margaret lived with their two babies, in a remote valley in Brazil. Harry was a teacher in a new rural Bible School and they lived in a little home which they privately called 'The House of a Thousand Fleas', for the last owner had kept pigs under the floor and rats visited them frequently.

But they were very happy, and warmly welcomed by their Brazilian neighbours. The babies toddled about in the sunshine and became almost as brown as their little friends.

Not far from their home was a deep ravine spanned by a rather precarious wooden bridge. Below it ran the river, from east to west, and the banks rose steep on either side. The southern bank sloped from cultivated fields and was a garden of beauty in spring. The sun shone on it all day long, and the deep roots of the plants bored down towards the water. A riot of glorious flowers cascaded down it, and the butterflies swarmed above them.

But the bank facing north was quite different. It bordered the jungle, and here the sun never shone and the roots of great trees drained the soil. Nothing grew here except slimy fungi - just roots and earth and the cold smell of decay.

Harry left home early one morning mounted on his mule. He had to ride into town and never had the morning seemed more beautiful. He watched the sunlight creeping down the mountains, chasing the shadows. Across the valley an ovenbird called to his mate and a praying-mantis beetle stood erect on a low rock as if praising God for such a morning. Already the women were down at the river washing their clothes and little white goats skipped in the pastures.

He was halfway across the bridge when he noticed the miracle - close to the bridge post on the north bank, where the sun never shone, was a perfect white flower. Among the rough roots and dark fungi it gleamed like a white star. Harry reined his mule to a branch and scrambled down the bank to investigate. He was no botanist, but he thought it was a kind of clematis. He lifted it gently and it came away from the earth at once. It had no root, only a frail tendril that twined round the post and clung to the boards on the lower side of the bridge. Such a frail tendril, so easily snapped, but it was doing its work. For over on the other side where the flowers bloomed and the birds sang and the sun shone, was the living root of the parent plant, pouring its sap into the tendril, reproducing its life in a cold climate - a beauty for all to admire.

And if that flower could have spoken it would have said this: 'I have no power of my own to bloom in this cold dark soil; but my life is linked with a life that blooms over yonder in the land of sunshine. I am part of the parent root; my flowers are like the flowers that bloom yonder. I have brought all the beauty of that life over into this sad dead place. I am a messenger from the land of sunshine.'

Author's Note: *Although we may have to live among sinful people who do wrong, we need not be like them. The Holy Spirit has brought the life of God into our hearts and linked us with Jesus. As this new life grows in us and we obey the voice of the Holy Spirit in our hearts and in the Bible, we shall become like Jesus, and those around us will see the love and truth and courage of Jesus shining out in the dark places of the earth. Your life will become like the life of Jesus.*

Keynote: Jesus said, 'Because I live, you also will live.' John 14.19

Your life is hidden with Christ in God. Colossians 3:3

Prayer: Thank you God that the Holy Spirit now lives in my heart, and I am truly sharing your life, linked with you. So I pray that today I may show out the life of Jesus :-
His love and kindness instead of my selfishness.
His purity when others speak of wrong things.
His truth in the place of deceit and dishonesty and lies.
So fill me with our Holy Spirit that Jesus may live again in me, in the place where I am today.

Think: The tendril was to this clematis what prayer is to your relationship with God.

The Work of the Holy Spirit
- his transforming power.
2 Corinthians 3:18; Romans 8:1–11

21. A HOME FOR VIRGINIA

It was an evil place where the miners camped and an evil life they lived. The settlement consisted of some broken down shacks, a couple of taverns, and every man carried a knife. Many of them were desperate characters who had good reasons for disappearing west with the digging gangs; and of all the settlements Roaring Camp was the most notorious for drunkenness, murder and general wickedness.

The nearest medical post was miles down the track so no one knew what to do when, one night, a tired girl on the point of collapse, staggered into the settlement and begged shelter. They laid her on a mattress in a deserted shack, and the girl closed her eyes and turned her face to the wall, while they went in search of help. But when they came back it was too late. The tired girl had died, leaving a wailing newborn daughter with no clue as to where she had come from or where she was going.

Once again no one knew what to do. They attended to her as best they could and buried her in soft earth down by the river and someone suggested putting the child on the next truck from the mine and sending it down to the nuns; but no truck was leaving for three days, and the baby was wailing bitterly. They were staring at it helplessly when, to everyone's surprise, old Charlie strode through the middle of the group, and picked up the dirty, wailing bundle.

'Leave her to me,' he said abruptly. 'I've reared a young 'un before now. You, Tom find the shepherd on the hill over yonder, and tell him to bring some milk mighty quick, and you, Jo, go down to the trading-store, and don't come back without a baby's bottle.'

The men were amazed. Charlie was probably the oldest man in the camp and his shack was if anything the dirtiest. Lonely, grizzled and despondent he seldom joined in the orgies of the young men. He would sit for hours staring out over the scarred landscape, chewing on his pipe. He seldom spoke, and no one knew where he came from or what he was fleeing from. A strange, remote character, old Charlie, and no one cared to cross him.

Charlie carried the tiny girl home and laid her on his dirty blanket. He stood for a while gazing at her hopelessly. He had had a baby daughter long ago, but his wife had left him and taken the child with her. He had not been sorry when his wife left, for they had learned to hate each other, but when little Virginia disappeared something in him had died. 'I'll call her Virginia,' he murmured. 'But my Virginia was clean as a white flower. Maybe I'd better wash her.'

With the aid of some firewood, a tinder box, a bucket and some lye soap the new Virginia was washed clean, but it did seem a pity to wrap a clean child in such a dirty blanket. Well, he had one clean linen shirt and a clean bit of towelling packed down somewhere in the bottom of his box. He wrapped her in these and walked up and down with her, trying to quiet her hungry cries until the shepherd arrived with some ewe's milk. It would take many hours to procure a bottle, so he tore off a strip of towelling, dipped it in the milk and let her suck it. She soon fell asleep, replete and satisfied.

'She needs a cradle,' he muttered, resting his cheek on her downy head. He was beginning to love her. He had gold hidden down under the floorboards of his shack, and the shepherd had agreed to come every day. He laid her down gingerly on the blanket and went off to consult with the tavern-keeper, who produced an empty packing-case and some straw. At the medical centre they gave him plenty of white rags, and the trading store eventually produced a bottle and some baby clothes and a blanket. The whole settlement was getting interested now, and old Charlie's brat was fast becoming their mascot.

Charlie stood a few days later looking down at his new daughter. Truly, she lay there asleep like a fair white flower under her new clean blanket, with the white rags draped round the packing case. But somehow it looked all wrong, and for the first time he began to notice the filthy stains on the floor. It made the spotless cradle look out of place and for the first time he gave the boards a thorough scrubbing and they finished up quite a different colour. 'Now that cradle will look just fine,' he said triumphantly, lifting it back from the bed to the floor.

But now the floor looked all wrong and out of place, for he had never before noticed the clinging dirt and vermin on the walls, nor the black smoke-grimed ceiling. 'I'd best feed her and park her at Tom's,' he thought, 'and get down to the store. I need a brush and whitewash. I need summat to kill the vermin.'

He worked hard for two days, and one or two of his mates helped him while another minded Virginia, the innocent cause of all the disturbance. On the second evening he carried her proudly back to her rejuvenated home and held her on his knee. She seemed to stare round at the white walls and ceiling with solemn, baby-blue eyes and then she turned and stared unwinkingly at him, at his earth-and-tobacco stained clothes, his ragged beard, matted hair, and great dirty hands. He began to feel uneasy. He felt kind of uncomfortable in all this cleanness.

'Maybe I need to look in a mirror,' he mused, but he possessed no such thing. He laid her down and wandered off to the creek. Stooping forward, he gazed into the clear depths of a pool and chuckled. 'Kinda need sprucing up,' he muttered. The barber trimmed his hair and beard and he bought new clothes at the store. He washed out his old ones and laid them aside for digging, but he could not dig at present because he was too busy. He was glad for that little hoard of gold buried down under the loose floorboard.

So little Virginia thrived in her palace, kept scrupulously clean by her adoptive father, and as spring gave place to summer and the weather grew warmer he would carry her cradle out into the sunshine and she would kick and crow and smile up at the sky and the flying birds.

'But she'll soon be sitting up,' thought poor Charlie; 'and what'll she be a-looking at, with those baby blue eyes of hers a-staring? Trampled dirt and weeds, and an old trash heap! T'won't do!'

So Charlie started digging on his own path and the store produced some flower seeds. He went to the forest and cut stakes to erect a fence, while his baby crowed approval and gurgled. In the early sunshine and sweet mountain air his seeds grew fast, and by the time Virginia's curly head was peering over the top of the cradle, his garden was a place of greenness and beauty.

And other rough men saw the transformation and caught the idea. Gradually other little gardens sprang up, other shacks were cleaned and whitewashed. 'No reason for us all to live like hogs, is there?' asked the men.

No reason at all; but the real reason for the change was the tiny life of a baby washed clean in a bucket of water.

Author's Note: *When the Holy Spirit enters your heart, he creates a new, clean life within you. You can neglect it, or you can concentrate on it. Old Charlie made that new little life central to his home. Everything else had to conform to it, and what did not fit had to be changed. For us, this means placing:*

Christ in the centre, showing up what is wrong.
Christ in the centre, giving us the power to change.
Christ in the centre, transforming our lives
with his beauty and love.

Keynote: ... Set apart to become like his Son. Romans 8:29

Prayer: Oh Lord, I pray that this new life that you have given me be central, the most important thing of all. I pray that through constantly looking at Jesus I may see the things that are ugly and sinful. I pray that his Holy Spirit may so fill me that, because of the newborn life within me, my whole person may be transformed by the beauty and love of Jesus.

Think: Think of something wrong that the Holy Spirit has laid on your conscience recently. Are you using his power to put it right?

22. THE DEFACED LIKENESS

Young Sir Hugh was the first to see them coming; he was leaning on the gate, feeling miserable, as usual, when he suddenly looked up and recognised the cropped heads and sober attire of Cromwell's soldiers galloping between the young green wheat acres that surrounded his home.

It was the year 1649, and Sir Hugh had felt miserable ever since that cold January day, when a horse had come thundering up to the door, steaming with sweat, and the rider had flung himself from the saddle, and cried out the terrible news: King Charles had been executed at Whitehall, his son was in hiding, and their cause was lost. There had been a great deal more but Hugh, who was thirteen, had not stayed to hear it. He had run out into the garden, flung himself down under the wintersweet bush and wept and wept. When at last he wiped away his tears he noticed that the first snowdrops had pierced the oak mould. Thinking on this, he felt that perhaps all was not over. Perhaps, one day, there would be a new beginning?

He began to daydream about the Prince in hiding, often riding miles over the winter countryside peering at every young man he met, just in case; for it was rumoured that Charles was hiding somewhere in the West Country. So obsessed did he become with the idea of the outcast Prince seeking shelter in their Manor that he gave little heed to his Greek and Latin and his tutor was in despair. His father scolded him most sharply and threatened to cane him; but Hugh, after listening politely to all his father had to say, burst out eagerly,

'Good Sir, should we not get the attic prepared in readiness lest his majesty King Charles the Second should seek shelter here?'

His father's stern expression suddenly became sad and gentle. He understood now why his loyal young son could no longer keep his mind on his lessons. 'My son,' he said gravely, 'may God preserve the Prince and lead him to safety, but may God also preserve us from any such visitation. Would you want us all to follow our King to the scaffold? Are we not well known as loyalist supporters? Forget this thought quickly, child, and concentrate again on you studies.'

So Hugh said no more, for his father had changed. He had cropped his locks and laid aside his fine clothing and made Hugh do the same. They were now dressed as sober gentlemen farmers, and no one could tell for what party they stood, nor did they talk about the kingdom any longer. Yet the boy could not forget and he arranged his own little bedchamber with meticulous care, with a pile of clean linen, taken from the linen closet, always at hand, while on the wall before his bed he hung the small portrait of Charles the First that his father had purchased on his last visit to court - an exquisite likeness after the fashion of Van Dyck paintings. If the Prince came he would be glad to look on that.

But the Prince never came. Only on that April day a company of stern Roundhead soldiers came cantering through the bright countryside, making straight for his home.

Hugh slid from the gate and ran up the drive. He had very little time, for the riders had seen him and were galloping after him. He could hear the thudding of the horses' hooves on the path and he shot inside the door just as they drew up. But they still had to dismount and he reached his father alone.

'Good Sir, my father,' he gasped, 'they have come ... the Tyrant's men .. they will search the house and question you as they did Squire Robinson.'

'Then bid your mother hide the crested silver and all our Royalist clothing,' replied the father. 'Help her to cover all trace, while I detain them in the parlour.'

Hugh only reached his own little room a few paces ahead of the search party.

Already their boots were thumping on the stairs when he remembered - the picture on the wall. It was too late to hide it, and there was nowhere safe to put it. His father's voice drummed in his brain, 'Would you want us all to follow him to the scaffold?' He looked around wildly.

On his desk was a brush, a painter's palette and a half-finished landscape, for Hugh was a young artist. He seized the brush and daubed green paint on the King's face - a rough apple - blotches of purple on the beautiful jewelled tunic - a few plums - a smear of yellow for a plate, and Sir Hugh stood boldly in front of it, legs apart, guarding his King, when they entered the room.

They found nothing incriminating, but after they had left, Hugh gave the picture to his father who hid it away in a cupboard, and there it stayed, forgotten and undisturbed for many years. Sir Hugh grew to manhood and welcomed his Prince back to the throne of England. He served him faithfully for many years, and when he died his son and their descendants lived on at the Manor; and nearly three centuries later, one of them, who loved art, made the long hall into a picture gallery, and the little portrait hidden by those ugly daubs of paint was brought out into the light.

The heir to the Manor was puzzled. It seemed such a poor, insignificant painting but it was obviously old and the frame was beautiful, so it seemed worth keeping. He hung it high up in a dark corner, and , knowing nothing of its history, lost interest in it, until one day an eminent art dealer came down to see the collection. They paced the gallery together, stopping here and there, examining, discussing prices. The western sun shone through the window, and a bright beam luminated the strange little picture in the corner. The art dealer stopped short, peered intently, climbed onto a chair to look closer, and then spoke in a voice of suppressed excitement.

'Might I take down this small picture and examine it?' he asked.

'With pleasure,' answered the owner. 'I believe it has been in the family for many years and it's mid-seventeenth century; but I've never discovered what it's meant to be, or what is its history.'

'Have I your permission to take it and investigate it?' asked the dealer.

Permission was readily given, and late that night when his family were all asleep the dealer sat down to discover the mystery of the picture. He knew that those daubs had never been applied by the hand that had painted the rich, shadowed background. With palette knife and chemicals he peeled off the ugly yellow and green, and there, clear and lifelike, as on the day that it was painted, shone out the features of the King.

Author's Note: *When we receive Christ's Holy Spirit into our hearts, our bodies become dwelling-places of the Holy Spirit. The life and love of Jesus should therefore shine out with increasing brightness. But there are outward things that sometimes hide his glory and beauty, so that people cannot recognise Jesus living in us - carelessness, rudeness, slovenliness, bad temper and bad manners. Some people think that these don't matter, but anything that hides the character of Jesus matters to a Christian.*

Keynote: The God who said, 'Out of darkness the light shall shine!' is the same God who made his light shine in our hearts, to bring us the knowledge of God's glory shining in the face of Christ. 2 Corinthians 4:6

Prayer: 'Grant me the beauty of the inner man, and may the outer and the inner be at one.' (Based on a prayer of Socrates)

Let the beauty of Jesus be seen in me
All his wondrous compassion and purity

Oh thou Spirit divine
All my nature refine
Till the beauty of Jesus
be seen in me.

Think: In your own life, what are the bad or wrong things that you find most difficulty overcoming? Make a point of asking God daily for help with those, trusting him as the God of the impossible.

BUT THE SPIRIT PRODUCES LOVE, JOY, PEACE, PATIENCE, KINDNESS, GOODNESS, FAITHFULNESS, HUMILITY AND SELF-CONTROL. GALATIANS 5:22

23. A SURPRISE FOR THE BRIGAND CHIEF

Chang was a Chinese brigand chief in the days when foreigners could still enter China freely. He was head of a notorious band, well-known for its skill and wickedness.

The brigands lived in hide-outs in the rocks, high up in the mountains where the Government troops could never find them, and they would creep out on dark, windy nights, fully armed, to the boundaries of the villages. At a given signal they would all rush in at once, shooting down the fierce village dogs, grabbing or looting or shooting anyone who tried to resist them. They would sell the loot, little by little, in far markets and only attack again when they came to the end of their profits.

So, no village in the huge mountain ever felt safe, for no one had ever managed to overcome the brigands or track them down. But now a bigger scheme was afoot. Chang discussed the idea with his gang far up in the strongholds of the rock. They were an ugly crowd, and nearly all hated and feared their leader who always took the biggest share of the spoil. But most of them were hiding from prison or death sentences and dared not return to their old haunts; so they listened sullenly while Chang spoke.

He told them that the villages had yielded little loot of late, and they should be more ambitious. Down to the south at the foot of the hills was a small town. There were shops and riches to be grabbed in that little town, and best of all there was a small clinic run by three foreign devils. People came from all over the district to get medicine at that clinic and there were even a few beds for the very ill. Doctors, no doubt, were rich. There would be money in the hospital, and blankets and all sorts of paraphernalia used by foreign devils. They would get a great haul from that town.

The men listened sulkily. It was a much more risky project than any they had attempted before, but to rebel against their leader meant certain instant death. To attack at least only meant probable death. They lived continuously on the fringe of death, and it shadowed all their existence, but they knew of no other way of life, and blankets would be good in the cold mountain winter - if they were allowed to keep them.

The attack was planned for the night of the new moon, when it would be very dark, and a scout had already been into the market and made a plan of the lie of the land. They gathered round the rough charcoal sketch and everyone was told exactly what to do, where to go and what to attack; at the end all were to retreat instantly at the blast of Chang's whistle. The whole raid would only take a few minutes and Chang himself, with a few of the band, was to attack the hospital.

The night came and they attacked, and for the first few moments all went to plan. The night watchman at the hospital was quickly overpowered and Chang and his two companions burst into the quiet little ward, grabbing and looting , dazzling the eyes of the startled orderly with a bright lantern.

Just as they left, the foreign doctor came running out of the house with two white women behind him, but they too were quickly settled. Chang brought the flat of his sword down with such a blow on the doctor's outsretched arm that he could hear the bone crack, and the women were unarmed and shrank back at the glitter of the knife blade. Only as he put his lips to the whistle did he realise that something was wrong; the town had been ready for them this time, and the militia was installed.

A great battle was going on. There was shouting and screaming and terrified flying forms. Chang hesitated. He could pitch in and fight for his men, or he could drop his loot and disappear into the darkness of the trees behind the hospital.

He decided that this was a case of every man for himself, and he made off, flinging his lantern down at the base of the timber walls, for the excitement of a fire would cover his retreat.

Cursing, stumbling, bruised, he pushed on over heaps of rubbish, falling into foul ditches, struggling through thorny bushes, until the screams and clash of arms grew faint, and the blaze of fire made a red glow in the sky. Then he realised he was alone with the night and the silence of the hills. Alone, but not safe! At dawn they would patrol the hills, and he must get back to the mountain strongholds, the caves and rocks and the deep valleys.

Sunrise found him lying, worn out, in the shelter of the thickly wooded foothills - a terrified fugitive running for his life.

He was not caught. For days he journeyed on, crossing the mountains, begging in the villages and sometimes helping in the harvests, and no one suspected that this weary, footsore tramp was Chang, the Robber King, the terror of the countryside.

Yet he could not rest. Evil and selfish as he was, he had been the head of a band. He had tyrannised over them and cheated them, but now in his loneliness he longed for them. There had been no love lost between them, but in a strange way he had been proud of them.

How many had died in that battle? How many were taken by the militia? How many, besides himself, had escaped?

At last he could bear it no longer. The search must have been given up long ago, and even his own men could no longer recognise him, shaved and dressed as he was, like a poor coolie. He would go down to the town and make enquiries, and there in the plains he would seek employment, and perhaps, in time, purchase a little farm and a rice field. All love of fighting seemed to have died in him with the death of his gang. If there was any way of peace, he would seek for it.

He entered the town with the stream of villagers on a bright market-day, and strolled about noticing everything without appearing to look at anything. The hospital had not been rebuilt yet, and the foreign devils were not there. He stood surveying the ruins and began to question a local inhabitant.

'This is a pity. I hear it was a foreign house. How was it burnt down?'

'The cursed robbers came. They burned the dispensary and wounded our doctor. Now he is gone. But they surely will return and rebuild.'

'And what befell the cursed robbers? Were they slain as they deserved?'

'Many were slain, some were taken. Three were wounded and lay dying.'

'And what happened to those wounded dogs?'

'The militia would have dragged them away dying, but the doctor came out and pleaded for them. He said, 'Let them die here.'

'Pleaded for them? Why? Did he want to kill them himself?'

'Oh no! They preach a religion of love. The hospital was burnt down, but he took them into his house. His arm was broken and he could not do much himself but he told the women what to do.

The doctor went to another town and they put his arm in a plaster, but he was back next day. Day and night he watched over these three villains and cared for them as for his children. Those lions became lambs. One died, but two lived.'

'And where are they now? Did he hand them over to the militia?'

'Oh no. The militia counted them as dead and did not come back. When the doctor went away, those two went with him. They seemed like his sons. I do not think they will ever leave him.'

Chang could not believe it, and only when he heard this incredible story several times did it begin to dawn on him that this had actually happened. A man had loved his enemies, and done good to those that had attacked and robbed and burned, and the enemies had become friends. Love had proved stronger than the sword.

This had never before been heard of. This was no earthly love, born in the heart of men. That night, lying sleepless in the inn, Chang determined to search for the source of this love. The townsfolk had said that this was a religion of love, and there were others who held this religion.

He kept his resolve. Working at odd jobs and wandering from town to town he sought for the religion that made a man love his enemies; and there came a day when Chang found followers of Jesus and eagerly learned about the source of that love.

Author's Note: *For the source of forgiving love is God, and that loved streamed out to the world through Jesus. That same love is given to us through the Holy Spirit so that we can learn to love and forgive as God does. To know how God loved, read 1 John 4:7–21. To see how important this is, read 1 Corinthians 13.*

Keynote: For God has poured out his love into our hearts by means of the Holy Spirit, who is God's gift to us. Romans 5:5

Prayer: Love never fails, Love is pure gold,
            Love is what Jesus came to unfold.
         Make us more loving, Master, we pray,
         Help us remember, Love is your way.

Think: Jesus expressed God's principle of forgiveness perfectly in the Lord's prayer: 'Forgive us our sins as we forgive those who sin against us.' How can we put this into practice?

24. A SONG OF VICTORY

No-one really knows why Emperor Nero hated the early Christians in Rome so much. He had absolute power over the life and death of his subjects and they lived in terror of him; but these Christians did not live in terror of him for they had lost their fear of death. They knew that death itself could not separate them from the love of God, and to them, to die meant to make a joyful entrance into the presence of Christ and many of them were singing as they were being killed. They knew that Nero could kill their bodies, but he could not break their spirits, and perhaps this was one of the reasons why he hated them.

All through the summer Nero had enjoyed sitting in the Coliseum, the greatest open-air theatre ever built, entertaining himself and the populace of Rome by watching Christians being thrown to the wild beasts. But once the icy Roman winter had come, the Coliseum was closed, so what was to be done, Nero wondered, with a band of forty Christian citizens who had been discovered and arrested and were now awaiting the Emperor's pleasure?

'Let them freeze!' snarled Nero, looking out on the white winter landscape. He sent for a captain in his household guard to lead the forty prisoners to a small frozen lake in the hills above the city, strip them and send them out in the night on the ice to die or recant. The captain and his men were to light a huge fire on the bank and remain beside it until the last condemned traitor had either fallen, or walked back to the fire having denied his faith.

These were Nero's orders, so forty men stood together in the centre of the frozen lake under the moonlit sky. But now and again, above the crackling of the fire and the sizzling of roasting meat, a cry went up to the tingling stars- 'Forty wrestlers wrestling for you, oh Christ, winning for you the victory, claiming for you the crown.'

The captain listened in sorrowful silence for he too knew the way of Christ. He too believed that this way led to everlasting life, but he had never dared to confess it. He had seen too many suffer; how could he endure what they faced?

Then suddenly everyone fell silent and all faces turned to the lake; one stumbling figure was coming towards them, his head bowed in shame. For the fierce pain of the cold and the sight of that fire had proved too much for his endurance. The soldiers burst into mocking laughter, dragged him ashore, clothed him, fed him, and inwardly despised him.

But out on the ice the song of triumph faded. The group stood in heartbroken silence and there was no more singing.

And then once again the jesting group round the fire was struck dumb in blank astonishment and the laughter ceased. For their captain had risen, flung away his warm clothing, and strode out onto the ice, pale-faced and steadfast. And the group welcomed him with rejoicing while once again, through voices that were becoming weaker, the song ascended unto heaven -

'Forty wrestlers wrestling for you, oh Christ, winning for you the victory, claiming for you the crown.'

Keynote: Your presence fills me with joy and brings me pleasure forever. Psalm 16:11

Prayer: Oh Lord, I pray that whatever happens to me, I may remember that you are the source of my joy and that if I know you and love you, I can be happy in Jesus in spite of sadness or pain. Save me from grumbling, self-pity or depression and let me show those whom I meet that a

Christian is a positive person. Grant us the royalty of inward happiness and the serenity that comes from living close to you. Daily renew in us the sense of joy and let your eternal spirit dwell in our souls and bodies, filling us with light and gladness, so that we may meet all that comes, even death itself, with courage and peace, always giving you thanks in all things. Amen.

Think: Does your gratitude to God depend on your ups and downs? Or do you know what it is to 'rejoice in the Lord always'?

25. THE WINNING ENTRY

The students of an art class were having a discussion in the playground. Their exams were due at the end of term and each had to submit a painting.

A choice of subjects had been given and one of them was, 'Peace'.

'Quite a lot of scope there,' said one.

'A good seascape ... an early morning scene ... a sunset ...'

'But that's not very original!' said another. 'A night scene would be better, but night scenes are awfully difficult.'

'What about an old man surveying the fruits of his labours? Oh, but the expression on his face would need more skill than I possess. That wouldn't do either!'

'An animal study maybe. A cat curled up in the sunshine, but how do you draw a purr?'

'You could make it abstract - just a blending of colours.'

'Well, there may be endless possibilities, but all the same, I think I shall choose another subject!'

The examiner briefly sorted the entries into their subjects. A number of students had attempted the subject 'Peace', and he was rather bored with their efforts. The rather stiff figure stretched out on the beach in a bikini looked as though her joints were immoveable; the sunset sky was overdone, no one ever saw colours as lurid as that!

He sighed and turned over another and stopped. Had he made a mistake? Could this wild, tossing landscape be entitled 'Peace'.

He looked again and understood.

The young artist had painted a storm at sea. She had achieved the impression of scudding clouds and curling green billows breaking in foam over a pitching ship in the foreground. At the back of the ship crouched a few roughly sketched figures.

Yes, this girl could draw.

The attitudes portrayed terror, and some of the faces were lifted despairingly to the sky as though watching for some break in the storm.

But in the stern of the ship and right in the forefront of the picture, stood a larger figure drawn in great detail; a man stood braced against a cabin door, somewhat sheltered from the wind, looking down at the child he held so tight against his shoulder. And in the child's small lifted face there was neither fear nor distress. The storm might rage around him, but he was asleep in his father's arms.

Author's Note: *The peace that the world gives depends on blue skies, safe surroundings, freedom from fighting, disturbances and worry. But the peace that Jesus gives lasts right through the storms. Nothing can touch us nor hurt us without God having allowed it to happen for our benefit. To know and trust that he is in control whatever our situation, is to know peace.*

Keynote: Just before he died, Jesus said to his disciples, 'Peace is what I leave with you; it is my own peace that I give you. I do not give it as the world does. Do not be worried and upset. Do not be afraid.' John 14:27

Prayer: Drop your still dews of quietness,
                Till all our striving cease
            Take from our souls the strain and stress
              And let our ordered lives confess
                The beauty of your peace.

Think: Just as a young plant needs nourishment, water, sun and rain, to grow and be healthy so you need 'spiritual' food to grow as a Christian. Here are a few helpful points for deepening your faith:

* *God's voice* - God speaks to us in a variety of ways, but one important way is through the Bible.

Prayer - Prayer is not a shopping list of daily requests. Prayer should be a way of life - by living constantly in the awareness of God's presence, being open to him and talking with him throughout the day.

* *Serving God* - Try to find out how you can serve God best, giving special thought to the kind of person you are, the natural gifts and abilities God has given you and the time and opportunities you have.

* *Christian Support* - To join a church, Sunday School or Youth Group would probably be a great help and encouragement to you, but would also put you in situations where you could help others.

* *Purity of heart*- if you sin, ask forgiveness and put it right quickly, thus keeping your conscience clear.

* *Your Faith in God* - needs to grow. When in difficulty, look to God's supreme power and his love for you, rather than the size of your problem.

SPIRITUAL GROWTH
I - RELATIONSHIP WITH GOD

26. THE BOOK IN THE BEDSIDE CUPBOARD

Moshe was a French-born Jew and all through his childhood he had been taken to the synagogue, Sabbath by Sabbath, and heard the Old Testament read. His father was a wealthy businessman and deeply religious, and like all other orthodox Jews he awaited the coming of their promised Messiah. He had never read of Jesus who fulfilled all that was written in the Old Testament about the one who should come.

Moshe loved and honoured his father and eagerly awaited the day when he should become his partner in the firm. They often talked together and one day they got onto the subject of religion, and Moshe told his father of a classmate whom he particularly admired.

'He is the kindest, best boy that I know,' said Moshe, 'but he reads the New Testament and often talks about it. Dad, why is it so wrong to read the New Testament?'

His father instantly became agitated.

'My son,' he said, 'keep away from that book, for it tells a pack of lies. It tells that our Messiah has already come, and our nation failed to recognise him and crucified him. Moshe , I want you to promise me that you will never read that book.'

Moshe considered. The mystery of the book intrigued him. 'Never is a long time, dad,' he replied; 'but I promise you this. I will not open the New Testament until I am twenty-one. After that I feel I ought to judge for myself.' And with that his father had to be content.

Years passed and Moshe was twenty years old, a trusted young man in his father's firm, rising to a partnership. It was a proud day for him when his father sent him to England as the firm's representative to handle an important business deal.

Moshe had never been to England before although he spoke English fluently as well as three other languages, and London thrilled him.

When his business was finished he intended to stay on for a few days and see the sights. He booked in at a comfortable hotel and settled down in his room on the first evening to sort out his papers and prepare for his interviews.

But there is a Christian society in England and America called the Gideons, who put Bibles and Testaments in hospitals, hotels and other institutions. To Moshe's surprise on opening his bedside cupboard, he found a New Testament lying there! He shut the cupboard quickly and tried to forget it, but found it hard to concentrate on his business.

What was so dangerous and mysterious about the forbidden book? He longed to look but there were still a few months to go before his twenty-first birthday and his promise bound him. Yet all through his business appointments and sight-seeing, the thought haunted him. 'Why does my father hate and fear this book? What makes it so dangerous, so alluring?'

On the last night of his visit he could stand it no longer.

'My father had no right to bind me to this promise,' he said to himself. 'I am twenty and a man. I will read the first chapter only, and then I will fall asleep.'

His fingers trembled a little as he opened at the first chapter of Matthew, but as he read he was surprised and disappointed; it was merely a genealogical tree, a list of Old Testament names which he knew already. There was nothing dangerous or mysterious about this and he read on boldly nearly to the end of the chapter. Here there was a short account of the birth of Christ. He read more slowly. At verse 21 he stopped with a shock: 'You will name him Jesus - because he will save his people from their sins.'

Moshe read that verse again and again. Nothing in his old Jewish religion had told him that a man could be saved from his sins. He longed to do right and to keep God's law, but he knew that from childhood onwards he had broken it again and again, and he supposed he always would. Was there really someone who could save him from sinning, someone who could free him from that sense of guilt and enable him to be what he wanted to be? If so, he had found the answer to the biggest question in his life.

He shut the book, for he must not break his promise any further, but he could not sleep; he must know more. Next morning he travelled home, his business successfully accomplished, but somehow his father's proud congratulations failed to please him as much as he'd expected. Only later on, when the celebrations of his homecoming were over, did Moshe blurt out, 'Father, I have broken my promise, I read the Book.'

Moshe then had to face a very difficult time. His father made it clear that if he decided to become a Christian he could no longer remain in the firm or become a partner. Moshe waited until he was twenty-one and then, with a clear conscience, he started to study the book for hours on end. Through it God spoke to him and he recognised Christ as the Messiah of the Old Testament, the Son of God, his Saviour and the one to whom he owed everything. He left home and started to preach the gospel to his own people, the Jews.

I do not know the end of the story, or whether he was ever received back into his family. When I met him he was suffering loneliness and persecution, but deep down in his heart he was a happy man. For through the book he had found the real answer to life; he had found Jesus.

Keynote: Your word is a lamp to guide me and a light for my path. Psalm 119:105

Prayer: Open my eyes so that I may see the wonderful truths in your law. Psalm 119:18

Think: To read the Bible carefully, with the willingness to obey it and learn from it, is a most certain way of hearing God's voice. From Scripture you can also learn much about the person and character of God. This in turn can help you communicate with him in your daily life.

27. AISHA'S LETTER

Old Aisha lived in a village high among the rocks looking out over the Riff mountains. She had lived in that village all her life and except for an occasional trip to market, it was the only world she knew.

As a child she had tended the goats high up where the charcoal burners lit their fires among the scrub. As a girl she had later married, and travelled on horseback from the little thatched hut under the oak trees at the top of the village to another thatched hut under the oak trees at the bottom of the village; and here she ground corn and drew water everyday of her life, and here she had borne and brought up her children. But now her husband had died and her children had married and gone off to other villages, so old Aisha was left alone.

She was troubled because she seemed to be going blind, and whatever would happen to her then? Her daughters loved her but her sons-in-law did not want her in their homes, and besides, her own little home was dear to her. Perhaps something could be done about her eyesight. That night when her neighbours came back from the market, she tackled them on the subject.

They were quite encouraging. Yes, there was a missionary nurse in the little market town, and she had good medicine. Many went there and were cured of coughs and spots and sore eyes, and, no, she did not ask for money. Yes, old Aisha should certainly go, and they would take her on the mule when they next went to town.

Aisha went home comforted, sure that her sight would be restored.

A week later Aisha sat in the small mission dispensary,

peering round and waiting her turn. When it came, the nurse greeted her kindly, examined her eyes and told her to sit down again. When all the other patients had gone the nurse came and talked to her alone in her own language, and this was such a surprise to Aisha that it was quite a long time before she found herself able to listen to anything she said. But at last they found themselves communicating:

'I can't do anything for your eyes,' said the nurse. 'You need an operation. But my brother in the town on the coast is an eye doctor. I think he could make you see.'

'But how would I get to him?'

'In the bus.'

'But I've never been in the long distance buses and I have no money.'

'Perhaps your children would help you?'

'But if I did, what would I do when I got there? I've never been in the town and I would get lost.'

'You must ask your way to the hospital. Everyone knows the hospital.'

'And if I did get there, the doctor might not let me in. I'm only a poor old woman, and he won't fully understand my language.'

'He sees many poor old women every day, and he speaks your language. Besides, I will give you a letter telling him that you have come from far.'

The idea of a letter seemed to comfort her. She went back to the village and got in touch with her children. One day she arrived with her son-in-law who was going to buy her a ticket and put her on the bus, and another distant relative would meet her and lodge her. But she wanted that letter. She had great faith in that letter.

It was quite a long time before the nurse saw her again, and when at last she turned up she was hardly recognisable for she wore spectacles and walked confidently. The shuffling feet and the peering look had quite changed. She could see.

She arrived again in the middle of the dispensary, but again she waited until all had gone for she had a story to tell. So the nurse took her upstairs and, over a glass of mint tea, Aisha recounted her experiences, and the nurse smiled, imagining the scene - the busy outpatients department, the crowds at the door, the harassed doctor and the determined old woman.

'I went up early in the morning, as you said,' began Aisha, 'and as I said, I got lost. The relative with whom I stayed gave me money for the bus, but I got the wrong one and it was the time of the second prayer call when I arrived. The door was shut and there were many standing outside, late like me, and they knocked at that shut door. But the doorkeeper came out and told us that the room was full, and we must all go away and come back in the afternoon, or next day. No one else could come in. The people argued and some were angry, but it was no use. The door was shut.

But I held up my letter and I shouted in a loud voice, "but I come in the name of his sister; I come in the name of his sister."'

Aisha continued to tell her story. The doorkeeper had glanced at her letter. It seemed authentic and, for all he knew, it might be urgent. He admitted her and took her to the consulting room, and the doctor, recognising the writing, read the letter at once and glanced at her eyes. The condition was obvious and he told her that he would admit her at once. It was all a perfectly ordinary routine event, but to her it had seemed wonderful.

'The doorkeeper beckoned me in,' she continued with shining eyes, 'I alone! All the others had to go away. There were many waiting but he led me through the crowds in front of them all into the presence of the doctor. And I said again, 'I come in the name of your sister.' Many were waiting but he turned from them and took the letter from me and read it right there. And then he turned to me, who am old and poor, and he did for me all that you asked - a bed, an operation ... and now I can see.'

She paused and considered. When she spoke again her voice was soft and wondering. 'How precious is your name to him,' she murmured. 'He did for me all that you asked. How precious is your name.'

Author's Note: *'In the name of Jesus' is not a magic formula to have our prayers answered. As we have seen, it is Jesus's life, death and resurrection that have brought us back to God. It is because of what Jesus has done that we are again acceptable to God and can come to him through prayer. It is therefore through our faith in Jesus, because of our belief in him, that our prayers are heard. By praying 'in Jesus name', we are simply acknowledging to God, and reminding ourselves, that we owe our new relationship with God entirely to Jesus and his work. It also means that, just as the nurse asked for certain things for Aisha by letter, signed in her name, so we can ask and receive anything the Lord wants us to have, and this includes everything that he has promised us in the Bible.*

Keynote: Jesus... lives for ever to plead with God for them. Hebrews 7:25

And so he (Jesus) is able, now and always, to save those who come to God through him. Hebrews 7:25

Jesus said, 'I am telling you the truth: the Father will give

you anything you ask him for in my name.' John 16:23
Praying for others
Philippians 4:6,7; Colossians 4:2

28. THE RESCUE

Mark woke up early one Saturday and knew that summer had really come: the sunshine was so bright and the bird-song so urgent. He jumped out of bed and ran to the window. The world looked exactly as he had expected, fields sparkling and the mists tangled in the willow trees along the stream banks. Buttercups would shortly be wide open and there was no time to lose. Mark slipped on his clothes and tiptoed downstairs. He raised an eyebrow at the puppy who flopped out of his basket and followed him and they skipped out into the waking, breathing garden. He was glad it was Saturday and he need not be back in time for school. Everyone slept on later on Saturday so he had plenty of time before breakfast.

He hesitated by the gate. There were so many places to visit, it was hard to decide which to choose. He could climb the hill behind the house and chase the wild donkeys and look for larks' nests, or he could turn left into the bluebell woods and see if the hedge sparrow fledglings had flown yet. But in the end he decided to follow the road down into the valley and make his way along the stream bed to see how the frogspawn was getting on. The whole place should be hopping with baby frogs by now.

It was fun exploring the stream bank under tunnels of hazels, pushing through the cow parsley and sometimes using stepping-stones, while the puppy scampered in the grass above him. He was nearly at the frog pool, when he suddenly stopped, tripping over what laid on the bank, half hidden by grass and nettles.

It was a fawn cow, and Mark had almost trodden on top of her; she had obviously slipped and hurt herself quite

151

badly, for she lay very still, her head half in and half out of the water, her nostrils just above the surface. Her breathing was laboured and as the boy stood staring down at her, she gave a faint moo.

'Well she's alive anyhow,' thought Mark, 'and I simply must get her out somehow. She'll drown if her head sinks any further into the water.'

He climbed a little higher up the bank and took hold of her back legs and began to pull, but the great animal was far too heavy for him. She switched her muddy tail against his shirt and let out a low moan. Mark slipped off his sandals, rolled up his trousers and splashed into the stream. Perhaps he could lift her; he managed to raise the heavy head and rest it on a stone, but that was all, and she didn't like it at all. She rolled her eyes at him and struggled weakly.

'It's no use,' thought Mark sadly, 'I'm only hurting her. I can't do anything. She's far too heavy. And I don't know what mum will say about my clothes; they are covered with mud and sopping wet and all for nothing!'

He climbed up the bank again and emerged from the hazel trees into a buttercup meadow where other cows grazed. He picked up his puppy and looked around thoughtfully. 'Cows belong to somebody,' he said to himself. 'I can't see a house, but there must be a farmer somewhere. How silly of me to waste all that time. The farmer will know what to do if only I can find him.'

He climbed the golden slope, and there, sure enough, just over the top was a rambling farmhouse, surrounded by barns and smoke rising from the chimney.

The farmer was eating bacon and eggs with his wife in the kitchen when he heard a frantic banging on the front door. He opened it and found a wet, dirty and excited little boy hopping from one leg to the other on his doorstep and a puppy barking in the background.

'It's a cow,' gasped Mark, who had been running very hard. 'She's lying in a stream and her head's nearly under water. Please come quick.'

The farmer swilled down his mug of tea. 'Call Jim,' he said to his wife; 'I'll get a rope.. you show us the way, son.'

They were soon standing on the bank of the stream looking down at the poor creature. 'Best bring her up on the grass and look at her there,' said the farmer. 'Fix the rope round her front legs, Jim, and I'll see to her back.'

'Can I help?' asked Mark.

The farmer glanced at his hopeful face and smiled. 'Why yes,' he said. 'Seeing as you're so wet in any case, you might as well get down into the water and catch hold of her head.' So Mark crouched in the stream, and talked to the frightened cow and held her head, while the two strong men above him drew her gently up into the sunny meadow. And as Mark remembered his own hopeless little efforts he chuckled.

'And to think that the farmer was there all the time,' he thought. 'Why didn't I think to fetch him and tell him straightaway?'

Author's Note: *If we love the Lord and want to help other people, there are times when we really do not know what to do or how to help. But there is one thing that can never be wrong: we can always pray for those people and ask God to help them. He created them, loves them and knows exactly what they need. When we commit a person to God, he draws near to that person in a new way.*

Keynote: Don't worry about anything, but in all your prayers ask God for what you need, always asking him with a thankful heart. Philippians 4:6

Prayer: Father, I want to pray for my family and friends and especially for _____ who especially need your help. Father, draw near to them and bless them and teach them more about your love. And show me too if there is anything I could do to help them.

Think: Your prayers, however insignificant you may think they are, do affect the lives of others. When you pray for people, do you remember that God loves them, cares for them far more than you do, and do you expect God to help them? Have you sometimes considered that you might be the helper God has chosen for the very person that you are praying for?

29. WHAT MADE THE WALL FALL?

Lilias Trotter, a girl from a large family, was brought up in a beautiful home many years ago. But not till she was in her teens did anyone discover her marvellous gift of drawing and painting.

While spending a holiday in a hotel in Italy with her mother, she had been out sketching, and her mother, having heard that the famous art critic John Rushkin was staying in the same hotel, wrote him a note asking him to look at Lilias' drawings. He agreed rather unwillingly. He had always maintained that no woman could really paint. But what he saw made him change his mind.

He became her teacher and friend, convinced that the young Lilias was destined to become one of the greatest artists of the century. But he did not understand that art was not Lilias' greatest love, and was bitterly disappointed when, as a young woman, she gave up painting as a career. She went out to Algeria in North Africa to work among Moslem women and founded what later came to be called the Algiers Mission Band.

It was very hard work and she, who had loved beauty so much, started her life abroad in the slums and alleys of a large town. But she travelled too and loved the great spaces of the Sahara and often painted desert scenes. Over her bed hung a map of North Africa and she would spend many hours kneeling in front of it, praying for the scattered towns and villages of Algeria.

Only very few people listened to her message of the gospel and sometimes she felt discouraged. Sometimes she was tempted to ask, 'What is the good of praying? God does not seem to be answering and so few are coming to believe in Christ!' But one day something happened that taught her to keep praying because prayer is never wasted.

She was sleeping very early one morning in the house in the crowded alley when suddenly, without the slightest warning, the wall between her house and the next fell in with a crash. Mercifully she was not hit but her room was littered with dust and lath and plaster and she found herself staring into the narrow passage that divided her home from the baker's shop next door. She could not understand it for she had seen no crack in the wall. But she sent for the local builder and asked him to rebuild the wall and also to try and discover the cause of the collapse.

The builder, who was also something of an architect, took a good look at the damage and then went for a stroll outside; he came back quite excited. 'I have found the cause,' he said. 'I will tell you truly why your wall fell.'

He explained that under the baker's shop was a sort of stone cellar with an oven and a see-saw-like machine for kneading the bread. Every night the baker set this machine in motion and for over twenty years the nightly vibrations had shaken and weakened her wall, until that fateful early morning when the last vibration had done its work and the wall collapsed.

So the wall was rebuilt and the neighbourhood was most sympathetic and no doubt, urged her to sue the baker, but Lilias did not regret the incident for it had taught her something important.

She realised that her prayers had not been wasted. She was working in a stronghold of sin and suffering, but great wars are not won in a day. They are won inch by inch and blow by blow. Just as every vibration had weakened her wall, so every prayer prayed in the name of Jesus was weakening the stronghold, and she and the others with her went on praying daily. For they knew that one day, if they persevered and believed and endured the fortress would fall.

Author's Note: *The New Testament encourages us to put on the 'whole armour of God' and to fight against the powers of evil. The strongest weapon we have is prayer because it is through prayer above all that we keep in touch with God, using our own private and personal words.*

Keynote: At all times carry faith as a shield; for with it you will be able to put out all the burning arrows shot by the evil one . Do all this in prayer, asking for God's help. Pray on every occasion, as the Spirit leads. For this reason keep alert and never give up; pray always for all God's people. Ephesians 6:16,18

Prayer: Lord, you know that I often pray so long for something and nothing seems to happen. Help me to believe that every prayer prayed in your name is heard and achieves something, and in the end God's love and goodness will triumph over hate and sin. Keep me from giving up and becoming discouraged. Show me the things you want me to ask for, and then make me patient and steadfast and persevering in prayer.

Think: Why do you think God does not always answer prayer immediately? Although we may not realise it each time, God does in fact always answer prayer. But not necessarily in the way or at the time we expect. To some of our prayers, God answers, 'YES'. To some of our prayers, God answers, 'NO'. To some of our prayers, God answers, 'WAIT.' The next three accounts illustrate a 'Yes' answer.

30. SEASIDE HOLIDAY

It was their first visit to the seaside and it was all very, very exciting. They even had a special song which their mother had made up for them, with a chorus -
Little spades rattling
Buckets a-clattering
Off to the seaside are we!

The three eldest, aged six, four and three started packing days and days before they were due to go, although they usually unpacked again every morning.

Six and Four had a small battered attache case each and Three had a little basket. The baby had much more luggage than anyone else but it was packed for him.

When their mother found them enthusiastically packing most of the toy cupboard and bookcase, she made one rule. Because they were travelling by train, luggage must be kept to the minimum, and each child could take one toy and one only, because, after all, they would be playing on the sand and in the sea and they would not need toys.

This caused some heart searching for Three, for all her dolls wanted to go to the sea, but none at all for Four because he had already decided that he would just take Eskie. None of his toys really mattered compared with Eskie, for Eskie was a part of the family. She had once been a handsome eskimo doll with a furry bundle of a baby on her back, but her early acquaintances would no longer have recognised her, for Eskie had had quite a life! She had travelled by post to Brazil and back to England in her owner's arms. She had been chewed, cuddled or laid on night after night, dragged out on expeditions, squashed in picnic baskets; she had fallen out of prams or been retrieved from the bath. She had long ago parted company with her baby and was really nothing more than a grey lump of mangy looking fur, but her faithful-hearted owner loved her just the same and never went anywhere without her.

The children thought Woolacombe the most wonderful place in the world, and for the parents too, the first week was a perfect holiday. The sun shone every day, and the children never tired of building sandcastles, exploring pools and running in and out of the sea. Every day they wheeled the pram to the beach after breakfast, taking a picnic lunch, and returned somewhere near bedtime, sandy and gloriously happy. But at the beginning of the second week, tragedy struck!

Eskie went to the beach daily with the family. She was usually propped in the picnic basket and left to admire the view, but on the day that they made the Great Sand Castle, Eskie sat in a little private sand castle of her own. The tide was coming in fast; the children were making a big barrier and Mummy and Daddy were helping. It was the most exciting thing they had ever done, for the waves were quite big and rough that day - large enough to knock over a tiny child if they suddenly broke through the wall. The children squealed with delight at each fresh onslaught and piled on the sand, and nobody noticed how the water was creeping up on either side of the castle, until mummy noticed the picnic basket about to set sail and ran to rescue it.

Of course the tide won the fight and three breathless, laughing children finally retreated, Three on her father's back. And it was only then that they realised that Eskie was gone. Her little castle had long been covered and the waves had carried her off.

Four was broken hearted. His father swam round and round searching but it was too rough to see the bottom and, anyhow, Eskie could have been carried right out to sea. There was nothing to be done but to go home.

Four choked back his sobs for he was a brave little boy. But he could hardly swallow his supper and when, just before bedtime, the children collected for evening prayers, he whispered that they should pray for Eskie. So Eskie was lovingly committed to God and they prayed that she would come back - after which Four seemed comforted and fell asleep.

Two days passed. Four was rather silent and spent much of his time on the beach searching pitifully up and down. His parents wondered how long his grief would last and for three nights they prayed together, as a family, that Eskie would come back.

On the third morning the usual procession started for the beach - Father, Mother, pram, baby, picnic basket, spades, buckets and three little children prancing eagerly ahead.

Suddenly they turned and ran back, for a large dog came bounding up the road dripping with sea water and apparently making straight for them. Three clasped Daddy's trousers and the other two got cautiously behind him.

On he came, with huge leaps, till he was close enough for Six to see that there was something in his mouth! The something was shapeless, grey and sodden, but the mother suddenly darted forward and seized it, and the dog let go and bounded on. There was a moment's dazed silence, and then cries of joy and laughter as Mummy placed Eskie in Four's arms and watched his sad brown eyes light up like stars.

And in case you say that this story is too good to be true, I can assure you that it is true. For I was Three.

Keynote: In their trouble they called on the Lord, and he saved them from their distress. Psalm 107:6

Prayer: Thank you, Lord for every prayer of mine to which you have said, 'Yes'. Thank you for everything I have asked for and you have given. Thank you for every time when I cried to you in trouble or illness and you helped me and healed me. Thank you that you care even about the little things and you love to give me what I ask for.

Think: Remember three things you have asked God for recently, when God has said 'Yes'. Was your prayer answered in the way you expected? Have you given God thanks?

31. THE RAINBOW PULLOVER

She stood at the door, one bare foot on top of the other, peering cautiously into the passage. A tiny dirty faced sister, tied on her back, slept against her shoulder and an older child clung to her hand. Out in the street the mountain drizzle soaked their rags, so they had come to school. Mfuddla, Sodea and Fatima lived in a hut with a flock of goats in a mountain village in North Africa. Their father had died, and every day their mother took the goats up into the ricks where they could find grazing. Early in the morning she sold the milk in the market place, gave the children some bread and turned them out to beg in the streets. The hut was locked until she returned with the flock in the evening, unless it rained very hard. Then she would come back sooner.

It wasn't very pleasant hanging about the streets all day, so when Mfuddla and Sodea heard that a school had been opened for children like them, they began to ask questions. What they heard seemed attractive. It was a strange sort of school. You turned up as soon as you had begged enough, but if you got there by ten, you got coffee, bread and olives. You learned knitting and reading and then the missionary who was also a nurse, told stories out of her book, and if you had spots or sore eyes or coughs (the sisters had all three between them) she gave you medicine. It sounded just right.

So Mfuddla, Sodea and Fatima became regular schoolgirls and always managed to arrive in time for breakfast. Mfuddla was very quick with her letters, and when Fatima cried on her back she would walk up and down, rocking her to and fro, chanting her alphabet. But what Mfuddla liked best was knitting. She was making a rainbow coloured pullover for Sodea from the scraps of bright wool that people sent from England, and if she hurried she might make one for Fatima and herself before another winter came round. She always put her little sisters first.

But otherwise she was rather selfish. If anyone took the ball of wool she wanted, she would stamp her bare foot and her eyes would flash. She tried to hide little balls of wool under cushions but they were usually discovered. The pullover grew in a glory of red, blue, white and yellow stripes and the thought of it brightened the shadowed little hut and the sacks that served as blankets.

Then, one Friday, the nurse made a terrible announcement: the wool was finished. They could come back on Monday for Bible stories, but the knitting would have to wait.

'Till when?' asked Mfuddla sharply, but the nurse did not know. There was no wool like that in the village and to buy it in the town for such a crowd would be much too expensive. It came in occasional parcels from friends in other countries, and the nurse's brother brought any parcels up once a month by car. She was expecting him in a fortnight's time, but whether or not he would bring any wool she could not say. Mfuddla would just have to wait.

But Mfuddla had no intention of waiting. She sat considering. Suddenly she looked up and said slowly, 'But you told us that Jesus Christ answers when we pray. So let us ask him to send us the wool by Monday.'

The nurse hesitated; how could the wool come by Monday? Parcels never came to the village. But she had no chance to say anything for Mfuddla was already arranging the children and the empty suitcase where the wool was kept. They knelt round it in a ragged little crowd, faces lifted, hands cupped to receive, as they were used to doing when they were begging. Quite simply, Mfuddla told the Lord that they needed the wool to finish their pullovers and would he be sure to send it by Monday morning. Then the school proceeded as usual, except that the nurse felt troubled. How could wool possibly come by Monday morning?

Just before the children went home there was a commotion in the street, a loud knocking at the door, and shouts of 'Telephone! Telephone!' For at the corner of the market was the house of a rich merchant and he owned a telephone. In an emergency he let the nurse use it, and now someone was asking for her. It was always an exciting occasion when this happened, and those in the street would run along behind her and wait at the great studded door to hear the news. The household inside would crowd round as she talked and want every word relayed. That day it was her brother who was waiting at the other end of the line.

'We can't come in a fortnight's time,' he sad, 'so we are coming tomorrow. Is there anything you need? I've just been down to the Customs and fetched a big parcel for you. It is full of balls of wool ... '

And when she got back and told the children the news, no one was very surprised.

'I told you so didn't I?' said Mfuddla. 'And I need some bright red wool, so please may I choose first?'

Keynote: Even before they finish praying to me, I will answer their prayers. Isaiah 65:24

Prayer:
Because you love me, Lord
And hear me when I pray
I'll tell you all I need
And trust you, Lord, today
Just as a mother loves
To give her children food
So you delight to give
All that is right and good.

Think: Practise speaking to God in your heart, telling him about your small needs at any time, and watching to see what he will do.

32. THE EMPTY BASKET

We met him in a strange and beautiful place, where for many years he was the keeper of the Garden Tomb in Jerusalem. There is a garden with a single old tomb cut in the face of the rock, and a single slab of stone inside where a body was once laid. Outside are the grooves of a great boulder which must once have been rolled across the entrance but there is no stone there now; the grave is open and empty, and because of its structure and position, many people think that it must be the tomb which Joseph of Arimathea gave for the burial of Jesus.

Many tourists come to see it, and Mr Maltar, the Arab guardian, used to love to show them round the quiet, beautifully kept garden and talk to them about the Gospel story. He invited us to a meal and we asked him how he and his wife had come to be in charge of this place, and whether he had been there long. So he told us his story.

Until the time of the Partition, when Jerusalem was divided into Arab and Jewish sections, Mr Maltar had been a bank manager; but when war broke out, he and his wife and his nine children were away from home, and unable to get back because of the fighting. His bank, his house and all his money were in an area allocated to the Jews and he and his family were stranded and fast becoming destitute.

'Daily I went to the branch of our bank in Jerusalem,' he said, 'but no money was coming through and they could not help me. At home we had lived comfortably, and my children had never lacked for anything, but in Jerusalem our money was running out fast. My wife and I were worried. Later relief was organised for the refugees, but just then all was in confusion. We did not know where to turn for help.

But daily we turned to the Lord. We read his promises to ourselves and we gathered our children and read the promises to them. We read in the Psalms, 'The young lions do lack and suffer hunger but those who seek the Lord will not be wanting any good thing.' We read in Isaiah, 'God's people will be free from worries and their homes peaceful and safe. How happy everyone will be with plenty of water for the crops and safe pasture...' Most of all we trusted the words of Jesus, 'Be concerned, above everything else, with the Kingdom of God and with what he requires of you, and he will provide you with all other things.' And I felt quite sure that God would keep his promises and we would not go hungry.

But I wanted my children to be sure of this too, and the day came when we finished the last of our food for breakfast, and once again I spoke to them. 'Children,' I said, 'the Lord has promised to give us what we need, but we have no money and no dinner. So we will tell this to the Lord and to no one else. And I will go out with this empty basket and you will stay at home. Then we shall see whether the promises of God are true or not.'

So we all prayed round the empty basket and the children understood that this was very important, and they watched me walk down the street with the empty basket in my hand. I did not know where to go, but I decided to look in at the branch of our bank again in case anything was coming through.

But the answer was the same as before. I turned to go, and found an old friend of mine from my home town in the queue. But he had left the district before and banked his money in Jerusalem.

'Why, Maltar,' said my friend, 'what are you doing here?'

'We have a small house in Jerusalem,' I replied, 'and we were on holiday. We were not able to get back.'

'Then you must be having money problems,' said my friend. 'Tell me, how are you managing?'

I was about to tell him of our plight when I remembered my words to the children. 'We will tell the Lord and no one else,' I had said. So I told him we were quite all right and left the bank with my empty basket. I did not know where to go next so I went and sat on a seat in the shade in the park opposite. 'I spoke the truth,' I thought to myself. 'Those who trust in God are always all right. All will be well.'

I sat staring at the ground waiting for a word or a sign. I did not hear when my friend walked toward me across the grass.

'I don't care what you say, Maltar. You can't be all right with nine kids to feed,' said my friend, and he dropped a handful of banknotes into the empty basket and went on his way. But I rose up and went to the market and filled the basket until it was almost too heavy to carry. I bought all that we needed for a good lunch and the rest of the money I put in my pocket. Then I went home. It was nearly lunchtime and the children were waiting at the gate, staring at the overflowing basket.

So we sat down together and ate our meal. It was good to eat so bountifully after the lean week that had passed, but it was even better to know that the Lord keeps his promises.'

Shortly after this Mr Maltar found work, and as his children grew up he and his wife retired to the little bungalow built in the Garden of the Resurrection. He became keeper of the tomb and the garden until the Six-Day War when he was shot dead, right by the open door of the grave. Perhaps he, who loved the place so much, would have been glad to die on the very same spot where his Master conquered death and the stone was rolled back. And still on Easter morning crowds throng into the garden to remember the Resurrection and to sing,

'Lies again our glorious King! Alleluia!
Where, oh Death, is now thy sting? Alleluia!'

Keynote: And with all his abundant wealth through Christ Jesus, my God will supply all your needs. Philippians 4:19

Prayer: Help me, Father, to believe day by day, your promises and to prove that they are true. I pray too for those who are needy and hungry in the world today. Give them today their daily bread. Teach them to turn in faith to you. Show me what I can do to help them.

Think: Do you *honestly* think that you would be happier or better off if God said 'Yes' to all your prayers?

33. THE BUS THAT WOULD NOT STOP

'Wake up, Fatima, we must be starting; the sun is already over the crest of the hill!'

Fatima yawned and sat up. She and Mary had been sleeping in the village where they went every Tuesday evening to give out medicine and to tell the Gospel message to any who wanted to hear. Menana, a woman whom Mary had first met in her dispensary, had begged them to come and had gladly welcomed them into her little home. So each week at sunset the thatched hut filled up with a crowd of dark-eyed villagers on their way home from the fields. Some just wanted medicine, but some would stay, crouched round the charcoal, and ask for Bible stories. Sometimes they would discuss a question far into the night and it was often after midnight when they lay down to sleep on the mattresses around the walls.

They had to be up early too and get back as fast as they could, for children arrived at about nine o'clock for lessons and their home was about eight miles away. Sometimes they walked the distance, but occasionally they caught a rather irregular market bus that would take them about three miles on their way, as far as a fork in the road.

That early summer morning they started off as usual. The harvest had been reaped and the fields were pale gold stubble, and the dawn wind stirred the threshing floors. Down by the river the Indian corn grew in emerald patches and the figs were ripe for picking. The sky was already bright through the early mists and it was going to be very hot. The sooner they got home the better. And to their great relief, the bus was in sight as they reached the main road - a bus laden with villagers. They managed to squeeze in.

171

Soon Fatima nudged her for they were getting near the fork in the road. They rose and battled their way to the front.

'Stop, please,' said Fatima. 'We want to get off here.'

But the driver turned out to be a very surly, unpleasant man.

'No,' he replied, 'I am not going to stop here. This is no proper stopping place. I'm going on to the next bridge. There is another fork there and you can walk back to your village.'

'But,' cried Mary, 'that will take us miles out of our way down the valley. It will take us hours to walk back up that steep mountainside. Oh, please stop!' And in her heart she cried to God, 'Oh Lord, we need to get home, and it is getting so hot. Please make him stop.'

But the driver would not be persuaded and there was nothing to do but to go and sit down again. Mary felt very cross indeed but Fatima was surprisingly calm. 'We prayed this morning that all would be well,' she said. 'We shall get back some time. Let us be patient.'

But Mary did not feel at all patient when at last the bus stopped and put them down at the foot of a steep hill seven miles from their home.

They stood gazing down the valley, in case another vehicle was coming but there was nothing in sight. Already the heat was shimmering on the hills, and the river, almost dried up now, trickled between the oleander bushes. They never heard the woman approaching. She had walked down the hill behind them, where they stood, and in her arms was a bundle covered with a cloth. She glanced at Mary, but went straight to Fatima.

'Is that the English nurse?' she demanded.

'Yes, my sister,' replied Fatima.

'Then present me to her,' said the woman.

She was a strong dark-eyed country woman in a shady straw hat, and a striped cloth round her waist. On her legs she wore leather gaiters to protect her from thorns and snake bites, and round her neck she wore charms to protect her from evil spirits. She came straight over to where Mary stood and drew the cloth away from the bundle in her arms. It was a baby and she had covered its face to keep the flies away from its infected eyes. The lids were swollen as large as purple grapes and stuck together. What the eyes were like underneath had yet to be discovered.

'I have brought her to you,' said the woman simply.

'How long has she been like that?' asked Mary.

'Four days. She lies crying with her face to the wall and will not suck.'

'But how did you know to come here? It is not market day. There are no others from your village on the road.'

'Last night I knew my child was getting worse. She was burning with fever. I slept with a heavy heart, and as I slept I dreamed. A man came to me dressed all in white and he said to me, "Take that child to the English nurse."

I said in my dream, "I do not know where she lives nor do I know her."

And the man in white answered, "Rise at dawn and go down to the main road by the bridge, and there you will find her waiting for you. She will tell you what to do." So I came and you are here.'

So they all set off up the long hill that led home and another bus soon came and picked them up. The woman stayed all day, and by evening, after penicillin injections and frequent irrigations the baby looked much better. Mary sent the mother away with medicine and promised to visit her on the Saturday.

The child recovered completely and that Saturday visit was only the first of many opportunities to speak to that family and village about the love of the Lord Jesus. The mother and her neighbour showed special interest, and Mary and Fatima sitting on the floor, telling them about the Saviour's love, thanked God many times over that he had said, 'Wait' when Mary had prayed that the bus would stop.

Author's Note: *Never doubt that God hears your prayer. If he does not answer at once, trust that he has some good reason. Read the story of Lazarus in John 11. They wanted Jesus to come at once but he waited for days in order to do a far greater miracle than healing a sick man. Many believed when they saw Lazarus raised from the dead, and what a lot Martha and Mary learned about Jesus in the waiting time!*

Keynote: Jesus answered him, 'You do not understand now what I am doing, but you will understand later.' John 13:7

Prayer: Lord, I would bring afresh to you those things for which I have prayed and seen no answer. Please strengthen my faith to know that you know and love and care, and that every prayer has been heard. Teach me to be patient and to wait your time, because you know best what is right for me. Thank you that one day I shall understand why you said 'Wait' or 'No'. But help me to trust you in the meantime, Father.

Think: Can you think of instances when a delayed answer to your prayer has finally brought about better results? Does this affect your trust in God about something you may have been praying for, for a long time now?

34. THE LOST LEADER

Everyone knew Stephen. He was one of the Christians and he had been made director of their Social Services, giving out food supplies to the widows. It hadn't been too well organised before, and they had had a few problems with the old ladies: the Greek immigrants had accused the Christians of racialism and of favouring the Hebrews. So Stephen had been put in charge of a small food distribution group, and since then there had been no more complaints. The widows were delighted and looked upon young Stephen as their father.

But food distribution was only a part-time job. Stephen's heart was burning with love for Jesus of Nazareth, recently crucified outside the city walls, the unrecognised Messiah of the Jews. But because he was God, even Joseph of Arimathea's stone sealed grave had not been able to hold him, and he had risen again and gone back to his Father. And before he went he had entrusted his disciples with this message - 'Go throughout the whole world and preach the Gospel to all mankind,' he had said, and Stephen, brokenhearted because he had been slow to recognise who Jesus was, and had not fought for his cause while he was still on the earth, now took every opportunity to preach the good news. No one could stop him. The moment the last widow had left and the place had been tidied up, Stephen was off!

Those were wonderful days; it was as though Christ lived again in his followers. His love and power shone out through Stephen. When he spoke, it was almost as though Jesus was speaking through him. But the proud rulers who had hated Jesus, hated him again in Stephen and tried to silence him by threats and arguments. When this failed they bribed false witnesses to tell lies about him. On their false evidence Stephen was arrested and taken into custody. Hundreds attended his trial and heard the lies that were told about him. His enemies watched him as he listened to their accusations, and they must have trembled and turned pale with awe, for God's glory shone out through Stephen. His face was radiant and shining, 'It is like an angel's face!' whispered one of the frightened people.

'Are these accusations true?' asked the High Priest, who was at least giving Stephen a chance to defend himself. If he was very tactful, very careful, he might yet escape. It was his last chance. 'But,' thought Stephen, looking round on that sea of angry, frightened faces, 'it is also my last chance to tell them of my living Lord Jesus. This is no time to be careful.' So casting caution to the winds, forgetful of his own safety, he made the long impassioned speech recorded in the seventh chapter of Acts, in the New Testament. He explained how one could trace Israel's refusal to listen to God's voice all though their national history, and also God's grace and mercy in always giving them a second chance. He told the assembly how now, God's great last offer to mankind had been spurned and crucified. There was, of course, still another provision - God's Holy Spirit, but Stephen never reached that point in his discourse. The mutterings were getting louder, and suddenly, grinding their teeth in fury and shaking their fists, the Jewish leaders surged forward.

But there were Christians in the crowd, and they were no doubt praying, 'Lord, save him; protect him; keep him from harm or death.'

Could there be a more terrifying situation? One man alone facing a howling mob out for his blood! But Stephen did not even appear to see them. He was gazing steadfastly upwards at the glory of God. The gate was open and Stephen looked right in. 'Look, Look!' he cried, 'I can see heaven open, and Jesus, like a man, standing at God's right hand.'

Perhaps the bystanders were gazing up too, but they only saw blue sky; however the rulers had had enough. Blocking their ears to drown that cry of triumph they grabbed hold of him. Pushed, kicked, punched, now on his feet, now on the ground, he was dragged outside the city. Flinging their coats at the feet of a man called Saul, his enemies began to hurl stones at him.

And the Christians no doubt cried, 'Oh Lord, save him from death! We need him! Keep him safe we pray.'

Stephen fell on his knees. The stones were coming thick and fast now, but the gate of heaven was still open. His master was standing to welcome him and he was almost home. 'Receive my spirit, Lord,' he cried, as a spent runner reaching the winning tape cries out for joy and victory. He was almost there; received into love; behind him there was atrocious evil and hatred. The love and forgiveness of Christ in him flowed back to them. 'Don't charge them for this, Lord,' he whispered, and falling to the ground he died.

The angry crowds dispersed. It was probably evening before the frightened, weeping Christians dared creep out to bury him. They had prayed for his safety, but he had died. God had not heard or answered - or had he? Could it be that, yes, their prayers had been heard all the time; that heaven's gate had been flung open in answer and Stephen gloriously saved and protected - saved from fear, saved from defeat, saved, above all, from hate? Had love not conquered right to the last so that, saved from death, Stephen now reigned in eternal life?

Back in his home, that proud Jew named Saul struggled with his fear and conscience and fought against God. He had been watching while guarding the clothes of those who had been stoning Stephen. Saul hated this Jesus. But tonight he was badly shaken ... What had Stephen seen? How could a man die like that in peace and love?

If the Christians had lost a leader through Stephen's death, God was preparing another one, for Saul was soon to yield to Christ.

Author's Note: *There can be several reasons why God sometimes says 'No' to our prayers. But it never means that he did not hear or that the request was not important enough. Usually God's 'No' means that 'Yes' would not have been right and good for us. But sometimes he says 'No' because he has a far better answer than the one asked for, as in this story. Many were helped by Stephen's life, but millions have been helped by Stephen's death. Although we cannot always see how things will work out at the time, we need to trust that one day we will understand and will praise God for having answered our prayer in his own way - the very best way.*

Keynote: I depend on God alone; I put my hope in him. He alone protects and saves me; he is my defender. Psalm 62:5,6

Prayer: Father, I want to tell you that I will trust you about the prayers that have not been answered. I trust that you hear and love me and know best. I trust that you are quietly working out a better answer than the one I wanted and I thank you that one day I shall understand.

Think: Do you feel let down when God answers 'No' to your prayer? Do you think that God has in fact let you down?

35. SONG AT MIDNIGHT

They leaned back against the rough stone wall and kept very still because the least movement was so painful, but also because their feet were firmly held in the stocks and it was almost impossible to move. It was pitch dark there in the heart of the prison, but the long agonising night was still ahead of them. What the morning might bring they had no idea, but it might well be execution. Yet they looked backwards rather than forwards, for their minds were full of the amazing, glorious and terrible events of the past few weeks.

They talked softly about all that had happened, glad that they were fettered close together. They remembered the day they had arrived at Philippi, two weary travellers uncertain of what to do next, but very sure that God had led them; .. then that quiet Sabbath morning when they had walked to the valley between the hills where the river flowed and found that little group of women praying, Lydia was amongst them.

Lydia! They had hardly had to explain anything, for Lydia's heart was already wide open to the truth about Jesus. She had been the first to believe and her home had quickly become a centre for preaching and hearing the gospel. Then others believed and little groups of Christians would gather there, eager for teaching. It had all seemed so bright until the incident of the slave girl, and that too had seemed such a wonderful victory for Jesus. The unclean spirit had been driven out of her, and she had become so gentle, so changed. But her masters were furious. No one paid to hear the evil spirit speak any longer. The girl had become a dead loss to them, and of course they blamed those pestilential teachers for the whole thing.

So Paul and Silas had suddenly been attacked in the street and dragged to the court house in the market place and accused of disturbing the peace. Nobody would listen to what they tried to say. They were simply beaten with rods there and then, and thrown into the town jail.

'Make absolutely sure they don't escape,' said the magistrates to the jailer. 'Strange things have been happening and you can't be too careful.'

'Oh, I'll be careful all right,' said the jailer. 'Nothing strange is going to happen in my prison, and I'll put their feet in the stocks for good measure.'

So there they were, stiff, sore, and bewildered, for it had all taken place so quickly. They did not really mind what happened to them. They were used to that sort of thing. But what about Lydia and the new Christians, and what about the newly-exorcised slave girl?

'We'll pray for them,' said Paul, for he knew that neither stocks nor bars nor stone ceilings could prevent prayer rising up to God. And as they prayed they forgot the pain and darkness, and Christ himself seemed to draw near and stand beside them in the cell, the Christ that had suffered far more even than they, whose voice had guided them to Philippi, whose power had saved Lydia and cast out the demon, whose healing, comforting love was round about them in the prison, and suddenly it all seemed so wonderful that they broke into singing. They just could not help it! Louder and louder rose those happy songs of praise, and the prisoners woke from sleep and sat up to listen, for no one had ever heard singing in that prison before. But more important, God was listening too, for there is great power in praise, and Satan cannot stand before it. As the music echoed through the prison, the foundations began to shake, bolts and locks were strained and iron doors flew open with a crash. Chains snapped and fell with a clatter to the ground and the frightened prisoners groped for the passages. They were suddenly free, but it was too dark to see which way to go.

No one was more frightened than the jailer, for he knew that if one prisoner escaped he would pay with his life. Roman execution was terrible and cruel. Far better die here now, alone in the night. He drew his sword to pierce his own heart and all his dark, evil life rose up before him. Where was he going? Could anything save him from the punishment of the gods?

Then a voice came clear through the darkness, 'Don't kill yourself! No one has escaped. We are all here.'

His fear increased. He knew that voice. It was the voice of the prisoner who had sung in the dark and who had not feared death. Perhaps those two had found the answer to death, and perhaps they would tell him their secret. 'Bring lights!' he screamed, and while the other prison officials ran in with lanterns and secured the cells he rushed to the place where the voice had spoken. Paul and Silas stood in the glow, masters of the situation, and the trembling jailer fell at their feet. 'Sirs,' he cried, 'what must I do to be saved?'

Strong and certain the answer rang out, 'Believe in the Lord Jesus Christ and you will be saved - you and your family.'

So there was the secret! There in the prison he washed their wounds and woke his sleeping family, for the time was short. And Paul and Silas, who must have been longing to lie down and rest, told them about Jesus and baptised them as Christians. Then the jailer took them to his home and they all had a meal together and rejoiced. It was a strange, wonderful night and the dawn came all too soon. The rumours were already all over the town and the frightened magistrates were apologising and beseeching Paul and Silas to leave the town at once.

Something very strange had indeed happened in the prison! And all because two prisoners had looked up to God in their pain and darkness and given thanks and praised him.

Author's Note: *Three simple key words can serve to remember three kinds of prayer - these are sorry, please and thank you. Sorry can stand for prayers of repentance. As we remember anything that has grieved or displeased God, we can ask him to forgive us. Please can stand for prayers of intercession, when we ask God for help and bring our own needs or the needs of others to him. Thank you can stand for prayers of praise and gratitude, when we remember all that God has done for us, for those we love, for the world, and we thank and praise him.*

Keynote: David's Prayer of Thanksgiving - Praise the Lord, my soul! All my being, praise his holy name! Praise the Lord my soul, and do not forget how kind he is. He forgives all my sins and heals all my diseases. He keeps me from the grave and blesses me with love and mercy. He fills my life with good things, so that I stay young and strong like an eagle. Psalm 103.1-5

Think: Try to write a prayer of thanksgiving in your own words, that you could keep and use again and again - thanking God for those things you are particularly grateful for, and maybe also, things you dislike but know to be good in themselves.

SPIRITUAL GROWTH
II – RELATIONSHIP WITH OTHERS

36. LI'S ROPE

He came limping along the street, his stick tapping, his begging bowl lifted and his nearly blind eyes peering at the light. He was incredibly ragged, dirty and footsore and he seemed lost. Where the road divided he stood still.

'Will someone lead me to the place of Heavenly Healing?' he called in his beggar's whine, and a child plucked at his sleeve and led him to the hospital gate. Tapping on the gate with his stick, he asked admittance.

'But the beds are all full,' said the gatekeeper.

'Then I will lie in the courtyard until one is empty,' said poor Li. 'Only you must feed me, for I have come many, many miles seeing only the light ahead and the dust at my feet, begging and begging all the way. Many days I have been on the road, but all told me that I should find mercy here."

The gatekeeper shuffled off and fetched the doctor who came and looked at Li. It was quite true, the beds were all full, but the beggar's story sounded true. His feet were so bruised and calloused and he seemed so tired.

'Get him washed and put a mattress in the passageway,' said the doctor. So Li was admitted and for the first time in many years he slept on a mattress and was given good food three times a day. It was like heaven, and a few days later he went trustfully to the operating theatre and the cataracts were removed from his eyes. A little later the bandages were taken off and he was given a pair of spectacles. Li could see!

But there was more to it than that. A lonely outcast, Li had known nothing of love since his childhood. It was partly his longing for sight and partly the lure of the name, 'The Place of Heavenly Healing,' that had made him take that long, weary journey, sometimes bitten by dogs, often hungry. Now, evening by evening, after they had eaten their rice, they gathered round to sing and listen, and the story of the love of God revealed in Jesus seemed to answer all that Li had unconsciously been seeking. He felt as though his whole self, body, soul and spirit, had found the light of a new day. Truly, he had been healed.

He stayed for a long time; he could see and he should have gone, but although he gave up his bed to a sick man, he lingered on, camping in an outhouse and doing odd jobs. There was so much to learn, and those who taught him rejoiced at his understanding. Perhaps, later, he could train to be an evangelist. And then suddenly Li announced that he was going home.

When questioned, he was rather vague. They asked if he was going back to teach in his own village, but he did not think he knew enough to tell others. He only knew that he must go, but one day he would come back. Bowing with the greatest respect he left them early one morning, and those at the hospital watched him go rather sadly, for they did not think he would return.

It was many weeks later when Li came back. The village and hospital were quiet for it was the time of the afternoon siesta. Startled sleepers woke and ran to their doors at the sound of the tapping of sticks, and the gatekeeper glanced up, rubbed his eyes and started. Then he gave a gasp of horror and ran for the doctor. 'Come,' he cried, 'come and see! They are all heading for the hospital. What will you do with them all?'

The doctor ran to the door, his wife behind him. Down the road came Li, walking confidently, spectacles on nose. In his hand he held a rope, tied to the wrist of a blind beggar who shuffled along behind holding a begging bowl and stick. The rope on his wrist was attached to the wrist of another blind beggar, who in turn led another ... In all, there were some fifteen of them, for although Li had started off with three or four old comrades, they had picked up another in almost every village they had passed through, and the sad stumbling little procession had stirred people's pity and they had given them scraps of food.

'How could I not tell them?' said Li proudly, 'I who have seen the light!'

They rested and were fed in the shade of the tree in the hospital yard, and all were examined. Sad to say, not all could be healed but all heard of the love of Jesus, and some were admitted and regained their sight, or were given treatment to relieve their pain. It was a busy, difficult time for the doctor and the overworked hospital staff, but they were not sorry. For Li had come back and Li had surely understood what the Lord Jesus meant when he said to his disciples, 'Go throughout the whole world and preach the Gospel to all mankind.'

Author's Note: *If we believe we need to ask ourselves in the same way as Li, how can we keep silent? How can we not tell them - all our friends, who have not yet seen and received the light of the gospel? Jesus said that we are the light of the world, showing him to others as a lantern radiates the light that is shining within it. We who have seen the light, must tell others and show them Jesus by our loving and cheerful attitude. If asked why we are different we must be willing to tell what Jesus has done for us.*

Keynote: Help me to speak, Lord, and I will praise you. Psalm 51:15

Prayer: Father, I want to pray for my friends, and specially for those who are not interested in Jesus and who know nothing about the love of God. Show me how I can lead them to your light. Make me faithful in praying for them. Help me to live out Christ's love. When the opportunity comes, help me to tell them about the difference you have made to me.

Think: Think of a friend of yours who knows nothing about Jesus. Think of some way by which you could tell him or her.

Caring about the work of the Gospel.
Romans 10:6–18

37. THE GIRL WHO DIDN'T FORGET

Nicola had had a wonderful summer holiday, the best ever! Night after night, back in England, she would lie in bed and relive the joyful crowded hours.

In a way it hadn't been a holiday at all; it had been a working party - they had travelled out in a jeep and a Volkswagen van through France and Spain, crossed the Straits of Gibraltar in a boat, and landed in North Africa. There they had camped in two empty wards of a mission hospital (the patients had been sent home for a month) which they had redecorated. It had all been organised by their Bible Study leader, and they had joined two other groups, so Nicola had made a lot of new friends.

But it had not been all work. At midday, when the heat was almost overpowering, they would put down their tools, grab a picnic lunch, bundle into the cars and make for the beaches. Those vast Mediterranean beaches where the sand was too hot to walk barefoot, and where the water was so calm that they could see every pebble on the sandy bottom. Or sometimes they would drive further to where the great Atlantic breakers thudded on the shore and the surf picked them up like rag dolls and flung them back on the beach.

At five they did another spell of work - Nicola loved painting hospital lockers - and then they would take their supper into the garden, looking across at those amazing sunsets over the sea. Afterwards they would gather round to talk or to study their Bibles. Sometimes one of the hospital staff would come up and tell them about the work of the mission hospital, and some of these talks were unforgettable for Nicola. What must it be like, she wondered, to become a Christian and then to have your Bible torn up, or to be turned out of school or sent to prison because you were a Christian? And there was poverty too. What must it be like to see your baby hungry and not be able to buy milk for it? And what could one do to help?

One night one of the team had told about the summer camps they ran for some of these children. Different age groups came for a week each. In the morning they had Bible lessons and in the afternoon they went to the beach. Few boasted a bathing costume, and often they had to bathe in turns to make what was available go round.

It was nine months later, at the beginning of the summer term, that Nicola had her bright idea. And a month after that the worker in charge of the camps was talking to the children. They listened in dismay.

'You must all try to bring something to swim in,' she said. 'The old bathing costumes are worn out. Some I let you keep last year and there are hardly any left. If you can't produce something, you just won't be able to swim. You little ones, can't you swim in your pants?'

But the little girls were shocked and assured her that at seven years old it was not to be thought of.

There seemed no solution. Swimsuits were impossibly expensive, almost the price of some of the weekly family food allowances. They went home despondent, and those in charge prayed about the need. And then without any warning the parcel arrived with a letter enclosed.

'I don't suppose you'll remember me,' ran the letter, 'but I was in the summer working party last year, and you spoke to us one night. I just could not forget those children swimming in turns. At the beginning of the new term a lot of my friends turned out in new bikinis and I asked them what they'd done with their old swimsuits. When I explained I wanted them, half of the class produced old bathing things of some sort, so we send them with our love.' It was simply signed Nicky.

Oh Nicky, I wish you could have seen the riot that broke out when the children saw the contents of that parcel! It took some time to restore order. I wish you could have watched them skimming over the sands in their bright costumes or seen them listening quietly to the stories or singing the choruses! I wish you could have seen the wonder in their eyes when we told them we had prayed for a parcel.

You would have thought all the trouble of making that parcel and the heavy cost of the postage was so worthwhile. Thank you, Nicky!

Keynote: There are other sheep which belong to me that are not in this sheep fold. I must bring them, too; they will listen to my voice, and they will become one flock, with one shepherd. John 10:16

Prayer:
I know in distant countries
Across the deep blue sea
Are many other children
You love as you love me.
But they have never heard your name
And do not know that Jesus came.

Lord, help me send the message
Across the deep blue sea
To tell those other children
What you have done for me
Oh show me Lord, what I can do
That they may know and love you too.

Think: We do not always know what we sow, nor do we always see the result of our efforts. But so much can be reaped from even the smallest kind deed.

38. THE LORD'S WHITE CHICKEN

A story from Syria, where many years ago a young American couple set up their home in a country district and began to preach the Gospel.

The people in the villages round about were mostly farmers and shepherds. They had never read a Bible, nor did they know that their sins could be forgiven by trusting in Christ. These thing were wonderful to them and night after night, they would gather from the fields, tired, hot and earthy and sit and listen while Ralph taught them from the Bible. Many believed what they heard, and asked the Holy Spirit to come into their lives. One night as they talked about the love of God in giving Jesus and the love of Jesus in giving his life, one of them asked, 'But what can we give to show that we, too, love him?'

'We hardly have any money,' some replied, 'and what we have we must spend on our farming tools and our work. We all know that we live on our produce and are poor. Sometimes, in winter, we can scarcely even find bread for our children, so how and what can we give?'

Ralph turned to the book of Malachi and spoke of a time long ago when God told his people to bring a tenth of all that they had for the work of the Lord. But the people got lazy and greedy and were keeping everything for themselves. So the Prophet Malachi gave them a message from God. 'Bring the full amount of your tithes to the temple, so that there will be plenty of food there. Put me to the test and you will see that I will open the windows of heaven and pour out on you in abundance all kinds of good things.' Malachi 3:10

The group looked at each other. 'A tenth of our corn, our

eggs, our fruit?' they questioned doubtfully. 'But what if we haven't enough for ourselves?'

'What does the passage say?' asked Ralph.

'It says that the Lord will open the heavens and pour out an abundance of good things. It sounds good. But is it true?'

'Try it and see,' said Ralph.

So they tried. Each brought a tenth of their produce to Ralph, who bought it and either lived on it or sold it, and set the price of it aside. Soon there was enough money to buy building materials and they built a little church where they met to worship. Joy and blessing came to the village and it was easy to give. They longed to go to other villages to tell of their new found Saviour but they could not leave their flocks and fields. If they saved up more money perhaps they could pay for someone to go. The little store began to grow again.

And then there came a time of drought and gifts became fewer. Somehow the spirit of the little congregation seemed less joyful and the leaders of the church were troubled.

Someone else was troubled too. At a small farm nearby lived a widow. Her husband had died of typhoid fever, leaving her with three little children. Life was hard but she had a patch of land, a goat, and about thirty hens, and with these she eked out a living. But during the past year she had learned about Christ in her simple way, and life had been different since she had learned to take her needs to him in prayer.

It was a great day when she found her white hen sitting on a clutch of eggs. Instinctively she would have put one aside for the Lord, but 'better give the Lord a chicken that an egg,' she thought, and sure enough, a little later, ten beautiful yellow chicks hatched out. She caught one at once and tied a piece of sheep's wool round its leg.

'Why are you doing that?' asked her nine year old daughter Mariam.

'Because it is the Lord's chicken,' replied the mother, "and we must look after it carefully."

The chicks grew and Mariam loved them dearly.

'When are you going to give the Lord his chicken, my mother?' she asked.

'Not yet, my daughter. Let it grow; better give the Lord a hen than a chick.'

Then a very surprising thing happened. All the chickens grew fine and strong, but the Lord's chicken grew finer and stronger than all the rest. It was truly a prize chicken, its flesh so firm and its feathers so white. Mariam was glad , for to her it seemed right; but her mother was not glad at all. The crops were so poor in this year of drought, the wheat so stunted and the tomatoes so shrivelled. The Lord's chicken would have fetched an excellent price in the market.

'I was a fool to tie that sheep's wool round her leg,' she said to herself several times a day. 'After all, Mr Ralph only said a chicken. I could have given the Lord the scraggy dark one. No one would ever have known.'

And the matter so weighed upon her that early one Sunday morning she went out to the run and took the wool off the leg of the Lord's chicken and tied it on the leg of the scraggy one. Then she threw her veil over her head, spruced up her three children and set off to the new little church building for their communion services.

They did not always have a communion service at the end of their morning worship, but that Sunday they did. A Syrian Christian walked up to the plain wooden table where the bread and wine lay in memory of the body and blood of the Lord Jesus Christ, and before calling the people to come and partake, he gave out a hymn that had been translated into Arabic -

'I gave my life for you,
My precious blood I shed,
That you might ransomed be
And quickened from the dead
I gave my life for you,
What have you given for me?'

Sweetly and sadly the question at the end of each verse hung in the air. But before the hymn was over there was a disturbance in the church. The widow came to the front, her face buried in her hands, weeping bitterly, talking incoherently. But try as they might, no one could quite understand what she was trying to say. Only three oft repeated words were really intelligible - 'The Lord's chicken! The Lord's chicken!' And in the end it was Mariam who explained what the matter was with her mother. Running forward, shyness forgotten, she put her arm round her mother's waist.

'She says "Wait!"' whispered Mariam. 'Wait till she has been home. She wants to put the wool back on the leg of God's chicken. She doesn't want to take the bread and wine till she has done this.'

Nobody smiled. People were beginning to understand. The widow lifted her tear-stained face. 'He gave me so much,' she whispered. 'I only wanted to give him my worst. How can I remember him? Wait, oh wait ... I want to give him my best." Others rose quietly to their feet. God's Spirit was working.

'Brother Ralph,' said one, 'I too want to go home. I have not paid my tenth of wheat. How can I remember his giving?'

'Nor I,' murmured another. 'I feared the drought. I have not given milk to the Lord for many weeks.'

'Brothers and sisters,' said another, 'let us not take communion this morning. Perhaps many of us need to go home. Let us meet again this evening.' Everyone agreed, and then separated in silence.

Ralph got no rest that afternoon, for the people were queuing at the door with their gifts, and in the evening the church was overflowing. Joy and praise had come back to the village. Christ seemed so near and they were so happy. Mariam and her mother were there, and the widow's eyes were bright with tears as she remembered the love that gave all. Together they sang the hymn -

'Lord, let my life be given,
And every moment spent
For God, for souls, for heaven,
And all earth ties be rent.
You gave your all for me,
Now I give all to you.'

And down in the little farm, the Lord's white chicken strutted to and fro with a new piece of sheep's wool tied round its leg.

Keynote: Remember what the Lord Jesus said, 'There is more happiness in giving than receiving.' Acts 20:35

Prayer:

We thank you then our Father,
For all things bright and good,
The seed-time and the harvest,
Our life, our health, our food.
Accept the gifts we offer,
For all your love imparts,
And, what you most desire,
Our loving, thankful hearts.

Think: God always blesses those who give - whether it is their time, money, effort, or even their life. But God's rewards do not necessarily take the form we expect. If you want to give to God, be prepared to do so freely and willingly, out of love. Give without expecting anything in return, while fully trusting that God will bless you in his own time and in his own way.

39. THE BOY WHO FEARED THE LIGHT

It was nearly Christmas time and the weather was dark and stormy. Dave and Billy, hurrying home on the last day of term, longed to linger in front of the bright shop windows, but the street lamps were already lit and the lane leading up to the farm where they lived was full of ruts and puddles, so they knew they had better get home before it was completely dark.

'Come on, Billy,' urged Dave impatiently, but little Billy felt he was in fairyland. He got stuck in front of a window of a toyshop ... if only he could have that garage under the tree ... and a few of those dinky toys in his Christmas stocking. He had quite forgotten Dave who waited at the corner where they turned off from the main street into the lane.

And suddenly Dave noticed something that made him forget Billy. He was standing beside an enormous barrel of oranges, lovely and golden in the light of the street lamp. The owner of the barrel had his back to him, fixing a sign about Jaffas on the hoarding, and there was no one else there at all. It was getting near closing time and everyone was hurrying home to their teas, but the orangeman stayed on for the commuters on the later train.

Dave was all alone with hundreds of beautiful, shining Christmas oranges.

He put out his hand cautiously and tumbled three or four into his schoolbag. Nothing happened. He stuffed four into his pockets. No one had seen. He grabbed another five and stuffed them into his anorak. All was quiet and the stall keeper had not turned round. He just couldn't believe his luck.

But he realised that he was looking extremely fat and the quicker he got into the dark lane the better. Billy was approaching slowly, his eyes misty, seeing nothing but dinky cars, but even so ... Dave made a run for the high hedges and deep shadows. No one would notice his shape here. He would slip into the barn before entering the house and hide his treasure. Then he could go back whenever he liked, snuggle down in the soft dusty hay and eat oranges. It was going to be a wonderful Christmas.

Then Billy, who was afraid of the dark, gave a little cry of joy. 'Look! The lantern,' he shouted. 'Dad's coming to meet us!'

Billy ran forward. Dave froze. 'You there?' called their father. 'Dark's coming early tonight and you'll be falling into the puddles. Come and walk by me, Dave.'

Dave shrunk against the hedge, frightened and miserable. He had never thought of this horror. He could not face his upright, honest Dad, hugging his guilty secret. Billy was skipping along in the lantern light, holding his father's hand, all fear forgotten. But Dave slunk along behind.

'What's the matter, Dave?' called his father, who knew his little son so well. 'You've been a bad boy today?'

'Dave's been good today,' said Billy loyally. 'Teacher said he was the best runner in the class. Dad, you know my sock ...'

'Dave, come here and walk in the light. You'll stumble there in the ditch.'

'I'm OK Dad.'

'Now don't be daft, Dave! You'll get your shoes in a terrible muck ...'

'I like walking here ... oh! ...ow!' Dave had caught his foot in a root and gone flat on his nose. The oranges rolled out of his bag in all directions and the ones in his anorak squashed with a horrible squelch. His father stepped back to the side of the lane and lifted the lantern. Dave burst into wild, frightened sobs.

'I see!' said his father grimly. He picked Dave up and stood him in the light. His hands and knees were badly grazed, his mouth was full of gravel and his lip was bleeding. He looked so wretched and scared that his father wondered if perhaps he'd been punished enough.

'You took them from Sam Smith's stall, didn't you?' said the farmer.

'Y...Y...Yes,' sobbed Dave.

'You're a thief, Dave, and you're going back right now to pay for them.'

'But...but...I haven't any money...and...and...he might call the police!'

'That's up to him. If Sam Smith calls the police it's no more than you deserve. For the moment, here is some money. You go right back and tell Sam what you did and ask how much a dozen oranges cost. Bill and I will wait for you at the corner.'

Sam was very surprised when a terrified, dirty-faced little boy suddenly appeared out of the dark and sobbed out his story. He took the money and told him that if he caught him at such tricks again, he'd call the police at once. When Dave had turned away Sam winked broadly at the farmer who was standing under the next street lamp.

And then suddenly it was all over. Of course he would have to pay back from his pocket money, but somehow that did not matter much. The oranges were paid for and he was forgiven. He was limping up the lane by the light of the lantern, sniffing and hiccuping and very sore, but his father's arm was round him, helping him over the puddles.

Never do such a thing like that again, Dave, said his father. It just doesn't pay. See?

And Dave, clinging to his Dad, vowed that he never, never would.

Author's Note: *If we sin, we cannot walk in the light with Jesus. When you know there is something on your conscience, you need to confess it and put it right with God quickly. Then you will be cleared and forgiven, and will come back to walk with Jesus.*

Keynote: Jesus said, 'I have come into the world as light, so that everyone who believes in me should not remain in the darkness.' John 12:46

The light has come into the world, but people love darkness rather than light, because their deeds are evil. John 3:19

If we live in the light - as he is in the light - then we have fellowship with one another, and the blood of Jesus, his Son, purifies us from all sin. 1 John 1:7

Prayer: Oh Lord, I pray that I may never allow unconfessed sin to come between me and you. Keep me walking in the light with Jesus with nothing to hide. Keep me close to Jesus.

'Teach me to stand to
my own conscience clear;
Help me to be the thing that I appear.'

Think: No sin is too small or too great for God's forgiving love.

40. OUT OF THE FIRE

Jonathan had become a Christian at camp, but he did not feel he was getting on very well. At first he had felt so happy and had enjoyed learning from his Bible and his Daily Notes and had found it easy to pray. It was all new and exciting, and he was more helpful at home, easier to get on with, kinder and more careful about what he said.

But it did not last. The mornings were getting colder and it was harder to get up, and he was finding his daily Bible reading and prayer rather a bore. He had made friends with a boy in school who laughed at religion and Jonathan felt lonely and disappointed. Perhaps, he thought, he had just imagined all that happened at camp; perhaps there had been nothing real about it.

But before he completely gave it up, he decided to visit a certain old man, the grandfather of some boys who had invited him to camp. The two families occasionally visited each other. Jonathan had once heard him speak in a church and had felt rather vaguely that here was someone who knew God. He was a gentle old man with kind blue eyes and Jonathan felt he might be able to talk to him. He phoned him up and was invited over for tea.

He felt rather nervous as he cycled up to the gate and unsure of what he would say, or even if there was anything to say. But the old man was very welcoming, and drew up two chairs in front of the old-fashioned blazing coal fire, while his wife brought in tea. Melted by the warmth and the hot buttered toast, Jonathan found that he could discuss his troubles quite easily and they talked for a long time. Then suddenly, the old man said,

'What about your church? Its members should be helping

you and praying for you. Have you talked all this over with your Vicar or Pastor?'

Jonathan looked embarrassed. 'Well, to be honest,' he said at last, 'I don't usually go to church. My family only go at Christmas and Easter, and Sunday is a very busy day for me. I'm working for 'O' levels and I need the weekends to get on with other things. Besides, I did go once or twice and I found it rather boring. I try and read my Bible a bit extra on Sundays, and sometimes I go for a walk in the country, but I haven't done anything about church.'

The old man seemed to be thinking. Then he took up the tongs and leaned forward and picked one glowing coal out of the fire and laid it carefully by itself on the grate. 'Watch that coal," he said quietly, "and tell me what happens to it.'

Jonathan stared at the white-hot, glowing particle and saw the glow fade under his eyes. Red gave way to dull grey and the light disappeared and the heat grew cold. Then the old man picked it up again and put it back into the blaze. 'Watch it again,' he said.

And the dull grey lump was kindled, caught alight and became part of the glowing heart of the fire.

Then the old man explained that Christians were never meant to go it alone, any more than a soldier can fight a war alone, or a hand or a foot can function alone. 'The soldier is part of an army,' he said, 'and the hand is part of a body. When you became a Christian you became part of a body - the real Church which consists of everyone in every country who loves Jesus, but who, for convenience sake, meet in different buildings and worship in different ways. They are nevertheless all one in the eyes of God. By yourself you are at risk of growing cold, but gathered with other Christians, learning, sharing, giving and praying together, your faith will be strengthened, your love will grow warm and your light will shine.'

As Jonathan cycled home that night he decided not to let another Sunday pass without finding a church where people loved Jesus and learned together and prayed together, for he had realised his need for getting back into the heart of the fire.

Author's Note: *Some people enjoy company more than others. You might be a loner rather than a sociable person, and therefore tend to feel shy and uneasy in a group of people. You will nevertheless be greatly helped in your Christian life by becoming a part of some sort of Christian group - a youth group, Sunday School or church fellowship with other youngsters. Perhaps it will not be easy to start with and it may take several weeks before you begin to relax and enjoy it. But stick to it, you will meet and befriend others with whom you have much in common - above all, your faith in Jesus, the same questions, problems and joys. You will find help and be able to help those around you.*

Keynote: Let us not give up the habit of meeting together, as some are doing. Hebrews 10:25

Prayer: Father, I pray for my church, and for those who teach and preach there. Help me to be faithful and regular in going to services, and help me to use Sunday rightly, remembering that it is your special day. I pray that week by week I may learn more about you, and that I may be a reliable member of my church. Please show me what I can do to help it. A prayer of Jesus: 'I pray that they may all be one. Father! May they be in us, just as you are in me and I am in you. May they be one, so that the world will believe that you sent me.' John 17:21

Think: Although you will personally benefit from it, remember that by joining a Christian group you can be a help and encouragement to others.

TRUSTING GOD - ON GOOD AND BAD DAYS

41. THE MATCHBOX AND THE COIN

A girl of twelve who lived in a country where Christians were abused and persecuted, was thinking of becoming a Christian, but she worried about the consequences. 'If I follow Christ, will he keep me safe and protect me from harm?' she wondered. Her friend picked up an empty matchbox and slipped a silver coin inside it. 'Look,' said her friend, 'the matchbox is like your body, the silver coin is like your spirit. If I fling this matchbox on the floor what happens to the silver piece?'

'Nothing; it will not be hurt.'

'And if I scrunch it up in my hand?'

'Well, the matchbox will break; but the silver coin will stay in your hand.'

'If I throw it in the fire?'

'The matchbox will burn; but not the coin I don't think. You could take it out again.'

'And which would you say is the most precious?'

'The silver coin, of course.'

'So in the same way, you can commit your body and spirit into the hands of Jesus, day by day. Your body may sometimes get hurt and one day it will die. But the *real* you, the important part of you, will never die. In the hands of the Lord Jesus you will be kept safe from fear and sin.'

Author's Note: *The Lord is able to protect us and keep us safe. No one can separate us from him, and nothing can hurt our bodies without God allowing it in love.*

Keynote: Jesus said, 'I tell you this so that you will have peace by being united to me. The world will make you suffer. But be brave! I have defeated the world!' John 16:33

Even if I go through the deepest darkness, I will not be afraid, Lord, for you are with me. Psalm 23:4

Prayer: Lord, you want my total commitment to you. I know that you want the very best for all of us. But I am afraid of pain and suffering or of being different. I am frightened of what you might ask of me. Help me to trust you more, and to really believe that anything that happens you have allowed out of love.

Think: To what extent does your faith in God and love for him fluctuate with your good and bad circumstances? How do you think your faith in Christ would be affected if a major crisis occurred in your life or that of your family?

42. THE GUARD THEY DARED NOT KILL

His name was Upton Westcott and he went out to Zaire as a young man, nearly a hundred years ago, to preach the Gospel to people who in those days were savages and cannibals. Later on, his wife died of backwater fever and Upton became blind. But still he stayed on, directing and organising what by then had become a large and flourishing mission. He died among the people he loved.

It was on one of his rare visits to England that he told this story. He was an old, white-haired man, but he walked so erect and fearlessly that it was hard to tell that he was blind. His eyes seemed to be looking back to those years long ago, when he was just a young man.

He and his friends had pitched their tent near a cluster of huts not far from the lake. It was a beautiful stretch of water but infested with hippos and crocodiles and behind their tent was the mysterious green border of the jungle. But the people were friendly and brought them bananas and other fruit, and when they had finished their hoeing and fishing for an evening, the villagers would come and squat round the fire and listen to what the young men had to tell them. Gradually a few came to realise that this message of love and eternal life was for them too, and one by one they cast off their heathen practices, and learned to live as Christians should - honestly, at peace with their neighbours, caring for one another.

They were very brave, those early African converts, for their lives had been haunted by evil spirits and it was hard to believe that this new, loving Father could really keep them safe. There was one witch doctor whom they had always specially feared, whose charms and magic were supposed to take effect all over the district. He was reported to be very angry when he heard that his people were turning to the true and living God, and all waited anxiously to see what his revenge would be.

It was supper time and the kraal was busy with its fires and bubbling clay pots, and Upton and his friends were also cooking when they saw the frightened boy beckoning from the margin of the jungle. They went to speak to him and found that he was trembling and his eyes were full of fear. 'I have come to warn you,' he whispered. 'You must escape tonight. My father will help you. He has a canoe ready and you must be down by the creek before the moon rises tonight. He says it is your only chance.'

'But why should we flee? Who is going to harm us?'

'Why, the great witch doctor. Tonight he sends his killers. At the darkest hour they will attack with spears. You cannot escape them.'

The three held a quick consultation. They had a gun for shooting wild beasts but they did not intend to use it for killing men, and besides, what use would it be if the tent was surrounded by spear throwers? Also, they had taught these young men and women to rely on God's protection, and they, the Christians, could not run away. In any case, they had nowhere to run to. Upton turned back to the frightened, waiting boy.

'Thank your father,' he said 'but tell him that our God has not told us to flee. We will trust in his protection and wait for what comes.'

The boy sped off and the three made ready for bed. They ate their supper as usual and the tropical night came swiftly. Never had they been so conscious of the rustle of leaves, snakes and birds or the soft distant chatter of monkeys. They sat for a time in the door of their tent, praying and waiting.

The moon rose, the world was flooded with silver light, but the three had no desire to go and lie down in the tent. Better, they thought to meet death in the open, seeing their enemies than to be cornered like rats in a trap. They had decided not to use the gun. What was the use of killing one or two in front, when six more would be throwing their spears from the back? And perhaps they remembered Stephen. He did not die with a gun. He looked up to Jesus.

All night they waited under the fierce tropical stars. Then the moon set. It was the cold eerie hour when mists rise from the lake and the world is shrouded. Perhaps now?

But no one came, and at last the sun rose and the tired young men, who had never expected to see another dawn on earth, watched the mists scatter with new eyes. Then came the sound of voices at the well, the crackling of fuel and the thud of hoes, and wreaths of smoke rose from the kraal. Never had life seemed so beautiful! They crawled into their tents and slept soundly, and the little group of Christians creeping up and peeping fearfully through the flaps, praised God and wondered, for had they not heard the news and mourned as those who had lost a father? Surely, the hand of the Lord had sheltered these teachers.

Months passed, and because no harm came to those who no longer worshipped the spirits, others took heart. Love and freedom were far better than the old bondage of fear. Besides, they were less afraid than they had been, for the old witch doctor seemed to have lost his power. Some said that he was too old and others said that the spirits had forsaken him. Whatever the reason, men feared him no more.

But all the same, Upton was very surprised one day to find the old man kneeling in the doorway of his tent, his finery drooping, his monkey tails flapping. When at last he bowed himself in, Upton saw that he looked weak and hollow eyed. 'I want to learn about the living God,' he said simply.

They talked for a long time. Upton spoke to him of sin and repentance and he seemed uneasy. There was so much sin; and there was one sin that weighed heavier on his conscience than any other.

'Then confess it that it may be forgiven,' said Upton.

So he told all. It was the night of the new moon, he said,

and he had sent his men through the jungle with spears and orders to kill the three, but they came back with their spears clean. They had shed no blood.

'But why?' asked Upton. 'We were unarmed. No one could have prevented them.'

'Because there were four of you,' said the witch doctor. 'My men had no order to kill four, and they could not see who was who. They waited till the mists rose but he did not go away. My friend, who was that man who sat with you all the night in the moonlight?'

But Upton could not answer that question. Had the Lord himself sat with them or had he sent his angel? He did not know. It was enough for him that they had seen the morning and that the old witch doctor himself was turning to the light of the Lord Jesus.

Keynote: His angel guards those who obey the Lord and rescues them from danger. Psalm 34:7

Even if I go through the deepest darkness, I will not be afraid, Lord, for you are with me. Your shepherd's rod and staff protect me. Psalm 23:4

Prayer: Thank you Lord for your care over me, all day and night. Thank you for any time in my life when I have been ill or in danger and you have saved and protected me. Keep, by your love and power, any who are in danger tonight - those who are unjustly imprisoned or who are suffering because they are Christians. May your love take away their fear, and may they be comforted and strengthened. Give them peace and courage today.

Think: It is easy to trust and praise God *because* of (pleasing) circumstances. It is much more difficult to trust and praise him *in spite* of (difficult) circumstances, but this sort of trust is specially pleasing to God.

43. THE HILL THEY COULD NOT CLIMB

This story took place during the civil war in Ruanda in the nineteen-sixties, when the members of one tribe rose up against another tribe. They marched through the countryside armed with axes, hoes and knives, killing, and burning the thatched kraals.

Inside the hospital precincts on the hilltop the African pastor and his wife and two English nurses, Doreen and Jo, were faced with a dilemma when they looked over the plain and saw little columns of smoke rising in the distance. They slept uneasily and woke in the early morning to see the glow of the flames in a ring round the bottom of the hill and knew that the murderers were very close.

Should they shelter the refugees from the burning kraals or not? To do so would be to take sides against the armed rebels and would almost certainly bring the whole band up the hill to plunder and murder not only the refugees but very probably, the patients in the hospital as well as those who sheltered them. But to refuse them might mean death to this crowd of about three hundred terrified people who were already swarming up the hill carrying little children and anything they had managed to snatch from the flames. Could this Christian hospital shut its doors and send them all back to the murderous valley and the fires? They decided that they could not, and the weeping, exhausted mob surged in to lodge in every corner of the house, the hospital and the church.

But now they were in real danger and they called a meeting of all their staff. They decided that the African pastor and Jo would leave in the car, under cover of darkness, and hope to get through to where help could be found, and the pastor's wife, Edreda, and Doreen would stay and face what came. Together they prayed for God's protection over the two in the car, for wisdom for the two left behind and for safety for the terrified crowds in the hospital. Then Doreen remembered a small picture that had been given her. It was the painting of a flock of sheep, some white and some black, with an angry snarling wolf trying to attack. But between the sheep and the wolf was a pierced hand stretched out, and nothing could get past that pierced hand.

As darkness fell the car set out to pick its way through the burning homesteads and rebel bands. Doreen tried to calm the fears of her guests and make them as comfortable and welcome as possible. At last, worn out, she went to bed. But on waking next morning, she ran to the window and there, sure enough, was the rabble army about to climb the hill, a terrifying mob of wild, armed men out for blood.

She had no idea what to do. The only possible course seemed persuasion. She called Edreda and together they walked down the hill to meet the rebels, and the men, amazed at such a show of fearlessness, halted.

Doreen spoke to them. She explained that they had no enemies, and their only function was to heal and tell out the love of God. Politely and firmly the leader replied that that was all very well, but they were harbouring enemies and unless certain men were handed over by nightfall they would attack the mission, capture the refugees and burn the buildings.

It was then that the voice that answered seemed to Doreen to belong to someone else. Astonished and unafraid, she heard herself saying, 'You cannot come up this hill; it is God's hill.'

A moment of stunned silence and then a boy, his eyes blazing with hate, thrust his face close to hers and shouted, 'There is no God, Mademoiselle.'

'Oh yes there is,' she heard herself saying, 'and you will see that he will not allow you to climb this hill. He is going to protect us.'

There was an angry muttering and a forward surge as some started to push past her, but the Hand was stretched out. The bandits faltered and fell back, and Doreen and Edreda turned and climbed the hill alone. But the danger was not yet over. She gathered the refugees and told them of the threats, and advised as many as possible to try and slip away when dusk fell and make for the Ugandan border. When she had spoken to them they prayed, and a great silence fell over the restless, frightened crowd as once again they claimed God's protection. But the silence was soon broken by the quick tap of raindrops on galvanised iron roofs and the rain came down in torrents. Mass attack through the liquid mud of the hillside would be impossible, and some began to sing for joy.

Later in the evening a bedraggled car chugged up the road through the floods and darkness. The pastor and Jo had got through and returned with authority to call on the militia to protect them. For the moment they were safe, and a few days later the refugees were slipped into government lorries and escorted over the Ugandan border to safety.

Keynote: A promise if you are not sure how to act - 'If any of you lack wisdom pray to God, who will give it; because God gives generously and graciously to all.' James 1:5

A promise if you are questioned about your beliefs - 'When they bring you to trial (i.e. question you about your faith), do not worry about what you will say or how you will say it; when the time comes, you will be given the words. For the words you will speak will not be yours; they will come from the Spirit of your Father speaking through you.' Matthew 10:19–20

Prayer: Lord, when I am in difficult situations and don't know how to act, give me your wisdom. When I have an opportunity to speak for you, and don't know what to say, give me your words. Keep me in close contact with yourself so that I can draw on your resources at any moment of need, and thank you that you are always there.

Think: God's weakness is more powerful than man's greatest strength. So why does God allow troubles and disappointment in our lives? Why do innocent people suffer? I once stood in a carpet factory and watched children weaving carpets that are famous all over the world. By their side lay bright threads and dark threads. The bright ones looked more attractive, but their swift little fingers used both. When I went round to the other side of the loom and saw the beautiful pattern unfolding, I understood why. The design would have been ruined without the dark background. Someone wrote this verse -

Not till the loom is silent,
and the shuttles cease to fly,
Will God unroll the canvas and explain the reason why,
The dark threads are as needful
in the weaver's skilful hand,
As the threads of gold and silver in the pattern he has planned.

The next story is when something dark and painful was used by God to make a beautiful pattern.

All things work together for good
Romans 8:28

44. THE BRIGHTER LIGHT

Like many shepherd boys, Mikhail may have longed for more schooling and adventure. A shepherd's life in the hills of Lebanon is not a very interesting one. But Mikhail was needed to lead the flock to pasture every morning, guard it through the long hours of the day and lead it home at night. This was how the boy spent much of his childhood, and would, no doubt, have spent much of the rest of his life had not something happened.

It seemed a perfectly ordinary day. Mikhail was wandering idly about, while the flock grazed, when he noticed a smooth shiny object half hidden by foliage and stooped down to examine it. Was it a smooth stone? He picked it up and what happened next he probably does not remember, for he had picked up an unexploded bomb. The next thing he knew was pain and darkness - many people hurrying round him, but always darkness, so that he could not tell if it was night or day.

But at last, when he came round and was able to think properly, he realised that he was in hospital, and it gradually dawned on him that it was going to be pitch dark for the rest of his life, for the bomb had destroyed both his eyes. It also dawned upon him that he had lost his right hand, but this loss must have seemed small with the loss of his sight. He felt he would never, never get over it and longed to die. When they took him home he lay down with his face to the wall and took no notice of anyone.

Visitors came in plenty to sympathise over the accident, and although he would barely speak to them he could hardly help hearing what they said. But nothing interested him until one day two ladies arrived who were strangers.

'We have come to offer him a place at the Blind School in Beirut,' said one of them, and she went on to talk about this extraordinary school. Boys apparently learned to read and work with their hands. It almost sounded as though they were happy, and Mikhail lay slumped in his corner, appearing to take no notice but actually listening to every word. It all sounded nonsense to him. How could a blind boy read and work and be happy? Blind boys lay with their faces to the wall and waited for life to end. There was nothing they could do. So the visitors left, but as they said goodbye they added quietly, 'If he will come, we promise him a place.'

Some time passed, and the subject of school was never mentioned again. But Mikhail thought of it nearly all the time, because in his long night, there was nothing much else to think about. Gradually he came to realise that by giving it a try he had nothing to lose. So one day he astonished his parents by turning and saying 'that Blind School in Beirut! You'd better take me there. That's where I want to go.'

So they made ready, and he and his parents travelled down from the hills to the great city by the sea, and they led him through the crowded streets. When they found the address and knocked on the door they must have all felt as nervous as each other, but they were very courteously received and led to a waiting room. As they passed through his parents caught glimpses of boys making baskets and cane chairs, boys studying, their fingers moving over the pages of great books, and yes, they looked happy! It was all most strange.

The master came to see them and listened to their story, but he looked very sadly at the silent boy who sat so still. When he had heard all he shook his head sorrowfully. 'It is impossible,' he said. 'You have come too late. All the places are full.'

But he had reckoned without the quiet boy. He suddenly looked up. 'You promised,' he cried bitterly. 'You *promised*!' And he pleaded tearfully for a chance. And the master, seeing that the boy was desperate, promised to fit him in somehow.

So Mikhail started off on what was to become his life work; for he himself is now the headmaster of the Blind School. From the beginning he refused to let his handicap hinder him, and he learned Braille reading almost as soon as the others with his left hand. Basket making was a problem at first but he overcame it by tucking the cane under his right arm, and the master often thanked God that he had accepted this eager, hard-working boy, whose expression gradually changed from one of dull despair to one of bright intelligence.

One evening, years later, the boys were gathered in the hall listening to a Bible talk. When it was over the speaker asked if any of the boys would like to share something they had learned. Mikhail rose to his feet.

'I want to thank God for my blindness,' he said simply, 'because without it, I should never have known the Light of the world.'

Keynote: We know that in all things God works for good with those who love him. Romans 8:28

Prayer: Lord, I want to thank you for the things you send into my life that seem hard and disappointing. Help me to believe that they too are part of the pattern. Keep me from grumbling and doubting. Keep me joyful and praising because I trust you.

Think: Can you look back to an unpleasant or painful event in your life and see now that a greater good has come out of it, than if it had not happened at all?

DEATH AND BEYOND - THIS WORLD AND BEYOND

45. BORN TO FLY

'Come on,' said the robin kindly. 'Can't you move a little quicker? The sun is shining on those leaves. I suppose you can't climb any higher, but at least you could feel its warmth on your back.'

'Yes,' agreed the caterpillar, eating its way slowly through a nettle leaf, 'I do enjoy the warmth. But as the sun occasionally shines in the ditch, I see no reason to go higher. I'm perfectly content with my quarters and there are some very good leaves down here.'

'Ditches! Leaves!' trilled the robin. 'If only you knew! Don't you ever long for sunlight and waving treetops and blue skies and birdsong and white clouds and wind?'

'Not really, dear,' said the caterpillar, 'although I'm sure it's all very nice. But I've always preferred green to blue and I never did like the wind. And as for swaying trees, I'd much rather keep still. It's far safer.'

The robin laughed.

'Well I suppose you can't help it,' he said gaily. 'But oh! I'm so glad, so very glad that I was born with wings.' He soared to the top of a swaying ash tree and hung there, singing and singing and singing.

The caterpillar reared herself up on her hind segments and listened for a long time. The happy song drifted down to her through the leaves. 'Wings!' she murmured to herself. 'I wonder!...' Her body suddenly felt tired and heavy and the limits of her sight very near. 'But I wasn't born for treetops and wide skies and the open spaces that they talk about... I don't even know what they look like. I was born for ditches and nettles and low plants and it's not a bad life either, while it lasts.' She continued to munch at her leaf and tried to feel content, but she was in a strange restless mood. 'I must be getting old,' she thought, 'or I wouldn't be feeling like this. Wings... wings!'

There was a tiny movement just above her and she looked up to see a fritillary butterfly perched on a michaelmas daisy for an airy moment, the sunshine filtering through her wings. The caterpillar thought she had never seen anything so light and beautiful and she suddenly became painfully conscious of her own heavy body. She wanted to hide, but it was too late. The butterfly had seen her and alighted right on her half munched nettle, and she forgot herself completely in the love and beauty of her visitor.

'Where have you come from?' she whispered. 'You don't belong in the ditch.'

'Neither do you,' laughed the butterfly. 'You're only a visitor here. You were born for the light, for wings and air and blue skies. I came to tell you.'

'I don't know what you are talking about,' gasped the caterpillar; 'and yet... sometimes I do have a strange feeling that I'm a stranger in this ditch ... There's something else ... but surely I, with my slow, heavy body, could never be like you. How could this ever be?'

'It does not yet appear what you will be,' breathed the butterfly, 'but I know that you are going to be like me. Don't forget. You weren't born for the ditch. It's only part of the journey. You were born to fly...' but her voice could be heard no longer for her wings had drifted out of sight and the caterpillar was left desolate, longing for her wings. She tried to munch several leaves but they tasted dull and insipid. Nothing seemed to comfort her. By evening she was worn out and curled up in the ditch that had been her home all her life. 'But I have a strange feeling that I shan't be here much longer,' she thought, just before she fell asleep. 'There's somewhere else!'

She slept and slept and slept. She wove a soft cocoon round herself which hardened into a chrysalis, and the rain and the falling autumn leaves covered her. Her neighbours in the ditch, the field mouse and the hedgehog and a whole commune of small earwigs thought that she had died, and they were sorry, for she had been a pleasant, well-behaved little caterpillar and they missed her.

But she wasn't dead; not in the least! One day she had a most extraordinary dream: something was calling her far, far away, but very urgently, like the chime of distant happy bells. But she was imprisoned and could not respond. 'I could never struggle out of this prison with my poor, soft, strengthless body,' she thought, 'and yet, if I don't answer this call, I know I shall die.'

And then she discovered she wasn't dreaming at all. She was struggling with a strength she had never possessed before and her shackles were breaking. She was pushing out into light and warmth and birdsong. She could not understand her own strength. It was like being born again. 'I'm different,' she whispered. 'My body is no longer heavy and slow. That call is somewhere far above me, but I am rising. I used to think that I should feel strange if I rose too far above the ditch, but I am no stranger to this sweet air. I feel completely fulfilled... This is what I was born for.'

She paused to rest on a bluebell and a charming blue butterfly joined her. 'Welcome to our company,' he remarked. 'I see your wings are scarcely unfolded. Allow me to show you the way to the buddleia. We are all over there.'

'Wings!' the little caterpillar nearly swooned. Who and what was she? She felt shy in the presence of this beautiful stranger, and fluttered awkwardly to the edge of the bird bath. Without knowing what she was doing she glanced down into the water and caught sight of her own reflection. She saw a magnificent red admiral with dark wings and red spots.

'Born to fly,' she whispered, 'born for the light'. And stretching her wings to full capacity she followed her bright guide to join the company in the buddleia tree.

Author's Note: *Because we are limited, we cannot know what perfection is. But the fact that we cannot imagine for example a perfect life after death, or a perfect body, does not make these things any less real. In our world, we can't see the millions of stars in the galaxies, yet we know that they are there.*

Keynote: This is how it will be when the dead are raised to life. When the body is buried, it is mortal; when raised, it will be immortal. When buried, it is ugly and weak; when raised, it will be beautiful and strong. When buried, it is physical; when raised it will be spiritual. We shall all be changed. 1 Corinthians 15:42–44, 51. Just as we wear the likeness of man made from earth, so we will wear the likeness of the Man from heaven. 1 Corinthians 15:49

Prayer: Thank you, Lord, for the joy and strength and beauty of those who have died trusting in Jesus, and thank you for the day when we shall all meet again.

Think: Jesus Christ is the turning point of history, having died, risen from the dead and shown himself alive again to men and women ... so death is not really the end. It is a new beginning.

46. FOOTSTEPS IN THE NIGHT

The master was going away and nobody quite knew why. It was all most interesting and the servants had plenty to talk about.

The master was young and unmarried, and some whispered that he intended to return with a bride. Others thought that he was off on some business deal that might take him overseas; for his wool, his wine and his wheat were well known all over the country. One thing only was sure, and that was that it would be a fairly long absence. He had given the bailiff exact instructions about the shearing and the harvesting, so he apparently intended to be away all summer; and he had also talked to the head vinedressers so he would probably not return till the early autumn. He had of course given clear directions about the running of the house. Everyone knew his job and would carry on as usual.

He left on a bright spring morning promising to come back soon, and the servants watched him ride down the valley with mixed feelings. He was a kind, just master and they all respected him, but he was a stickler for work and some of them rather liked the prospect of slacking off for a time. The bailiff was inclined to be lazy himself when the master was away and never bothered too much about how things were done. They wandered back to their jobs rather more slowly than usual.

Only one among them fought back his tears as he watched the tall, strong figure disappear from view among the cypress trees. Fidelis had been born a slave and had grown up in the power of a very evil master, overworked, half-starved and often savagely flogged. But his present master had once come to the house to trade and he had caught sight of the child, his

231

scarred body and terrified expression, and Fidelis had never forgotten the look of mingled compassion and fury that had burned in the visitor's eyes as he gazed at him. He had immediately asked to buy the boy, and paid a fantastic price for his freedom; for, being young and good looking, he was reckoned a valuable slave. Then this new master had lifted the trembling child up on to the horse in front of him with very gentle hands and comforted him with such reassuring words that by the time they had arrived home, Fidelis already loved the man who had rescued him. A deep, steady love had then grown with the years. His was quite a humble job: he swept the yards, looked after the watchdogs and slept near the great front door in case travellers arrived by night. But he worked for love of his master, and the joy of his life was to serve him and be near him, so Fidelis was usually happy.

Well, he could still serve him. The weeks would pass quickly if he worked hard, and when the master returned he was going to find the yards spotless and the dogs in fighting-fit, bouncing condition. He rolled up his sleeves and set to with such energy that the cook burst out laughing. 'Bless you boy!' she shouted. 'Anyone would think master was coming back tonight!'

The time really did pass quickly. The sheep were sheared somehow and the harvest gathered, and the wine pressed. Summer was nearly over and Fidelis often walked far down the valley in the cool of the evening, just in case... Surely he would come soon! He did not much care for the servants' quarters these days. Everyone was quarrelling and grumbling and gossiping about the enormous profits that the bailiff was making for himself in his master's absence. The bailiff himself was not often seen outside working hours, and it was whispered that he had moved into his master's private apartment and was entertaining his friends with his master's old wine.

The poplars turned gold and the first rains fell on the parched land and still the master did not come; and it was then that the rumours started. Travellers on the roads were few and it was generally accepted that he would not come till spring, if at all. Some said that he had gone overseas and no fool would cross the ocean now that the storms had set in. Others thought he had been attacked by brigands and all were gloomy and depressed. Now that the grape harvest was over and the wine vatted, those in charge had become lazy and drunken. Everyone did as he pleased and worked for his own ends. Only Fidelis remembered and worked for love.

Then one day there was an interesting announcement. The bailiff was inviting them all to a banquet in the main hall. It was some kind of celebration; and although no one knew what there was to celebrate, they supposed they would be told. Perhaps, thought Fidelis, he will announce the return of the master. He arrived at the banquet bright eyed with hope and excitement.

He looked round in amazement at the loaded trestles. Two of his master's sheep had been killed and stewed in honey, and the piles of sweetmeats and confectionery were surely made from his master's vats. Then the bailiff rose and hammered on the table, and amidst a deathly silence he announced that news had reached him of the master's death, and this banquet was a takeover. He was inviting them all to celebrate their new allegiance to himself.

Fortunately, Fidelis was sitting at the bottom of the table with the lowest of the menials, and no one saw him hurry from the room. He ran to his little straw pallet near the front door and wept and wept till he could weep no longer, and the great fierce watchdogs, sensing his misery, came and lay down beside him and nuzzled him; and this comforted him, for they, at least, had loved the master. The noise from the hall became louder as the night wore on and the servants emptied flagon after flagon, but Fidelis lay face downward and desolate, trying to decide what to do next. For never, never would he transfer his allegiance.

Then suddenly the great hound at his side tensed, and the one at his feet growled and lifted his head. Fidelis sat up and listened, but he could hear nothing but the shouts of drunken laughter from the hall.

And then the dogs started barking madly and made for the door and Fidelis seized their collars and tried to restrain them; but his hands were not strong enough for the dogs had heard that light, firm step and they knew. Out they streaked into the full moonlight and leaped upon the tall figure who stood by his horse in the courtyard, and then Fidelis knew too. He ran forward, and stood looking up at his master, his heart too full for speech.

'Down boys!' said the master. 'Quiet now!' and the dogs crouched and wagged their tails furiously. Then he looked down into the white tear-stained face lifted to his and knew that something was very wrong.

'Why, Fidelis,' he said kindly, 'is there only you to welcome me home? And what is all this noise that I hear, and why are the lights lit in the hall? And where are the other servants?'

'They are having a banquet master,' whispered Fidelis. 'They thought that you were dead.' And he sank down on the mounting-block and buried his face in his hands.

When the master spoke his voice was sad and grave. 'How comes it boy, that you alone are not at the banquet?'

And then Fidelis found his tongue. There in the quiet moonlight he poured out his heart.

'Didn't you pay that great price for me, master, and make me your servant? And didn't you promise to come back? How could I swear allegiance to another? Don't I belong to you, master? Am I not your servant for ever?'

He thought that one of the dogs had laid its nose on his head, but then he realised that it was his master's hand resting on his hair.

'Not a servant, Fidelis, but a son for ever,' said the master. 'Come, let us go in.'

Author's Note: *It often seems as though evil reigns in the world, but men have forgotten that Jesus promised to come back. Yet he gave many signs regarding his return, which have been recorded in the New Testament. Enough of these have been fulfilled for many Christians to think that the coming of Jesus is very near.*

Keynote: (Jesus said), 'After I go and prepare a place for you, I will come back and take you to myself, so that you will be where I am.' John 14:3 So then, you also must always be ready, because the Son of Man will come at an hour when you are not expecting him. Matthew 24:44)

Prayer: Thank you, Jesus, for your promise that you will come back and take your children home. Even though I do not know when this will be, teach me to live, ready and waiting for your coming. Thank you for the wonderful happiness that we shall know when we see you. 'He who gives his testimony to all this says, 'Yes indeed! I am coming soon!' Revelation 22:20. So be it, come, Lord Jesus!

Think: As Christians, we are called to be as diligent as if Christ were to return today, and as persevering as if he were to return in thousands of years.

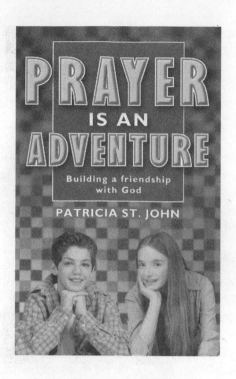

Prayer is an Adventure
by Patricia St. John

Prayer is a vital part of a child's relationship with God. It is something they must be taught to do for themselves and to enjoy for themselves. It is a two-way communication. We can speak to God who also speaks to us and we must listen.

ISBN: 978-1-85792-840-2

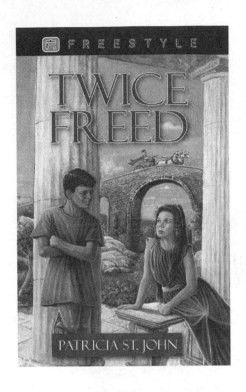

Twice Freed
by Patricia St. John

Patricia St. John's classic now back in print. A thrilling story of danger and faith with Onesimus, the runaway slave, in the 1st century AD.

ISBN: 978-1-84550-395-6

School Survival
by Catherine and Louise House

School is fab and friends are great too – most of the time but we can have problems and life can be difficult and often it's a fight just to survive! However, reading this book will help you. There is loads of advice and input and from people your age but God has some advice too. This book will point you straight to those parts of the Bible that will help you tackle tricky friendship issues, life and school.

ISBN 978-1-84550-353-6

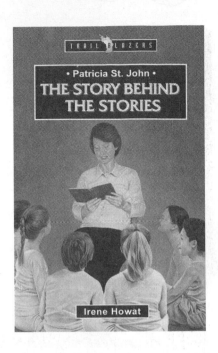

The Story Behind the Stories
by Irene Howat

Patricia St. John's life is a story in itself but she grew up to become one of the world's best-loved Christian writers for children. After almost being born in the middle of a storm on the Bay of Biscay, surviving the blitz in London she went on to work in a boarding school. Her exciting bedtime stories were favourites with the children! They were later to become her classic stories, *Tanglewood's Secret* and *Treasures of the Snow*! Every place that she called home was the inspiration for yet another story that brought children to understand and love their Lord Jesus Christ.

ISBN 978-1-84550-328-4

CHRISTIAN FOCUS PUBLICATIONS

Christian Focus | Christian Heritage | CF4K | Mentor

Christian Focus Publications publishes books for adults and children under its four main imprints: Christian Focus, Christian Heritage, CF4K and Mentor. Our books reflect that God's word is reliable and Jesus is the way to know him, and live for ever with him.

Our children's publication list includes a Sunday school curriculum that covers pre-school to early teens; puzzle and activity books. We also publish personal and family devotional titles, biographies and inspirational stories that children will love.

If you are looking for quality Bible teaching for children then we have an excellent range of Bible story and age specific theological books.

From pre-school to teenage fiction, we have it covered!

Find us at our web page:
www.christianfocus.com

CF4•K
Because you're never
too young to know Jesus